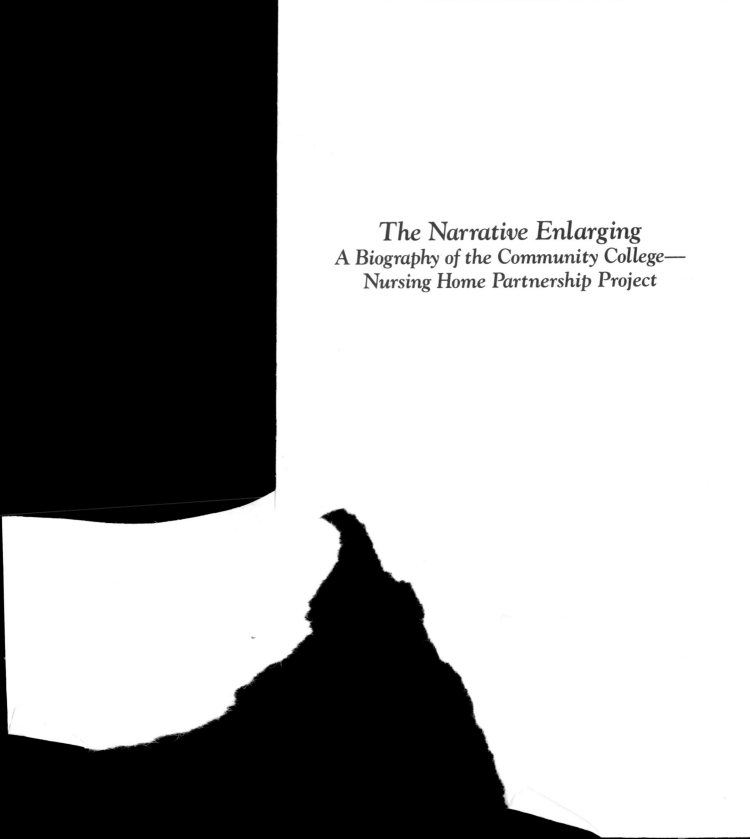

The Narrative Enlarging
A Biography of the Community College—
Nursing Home Partnership Project

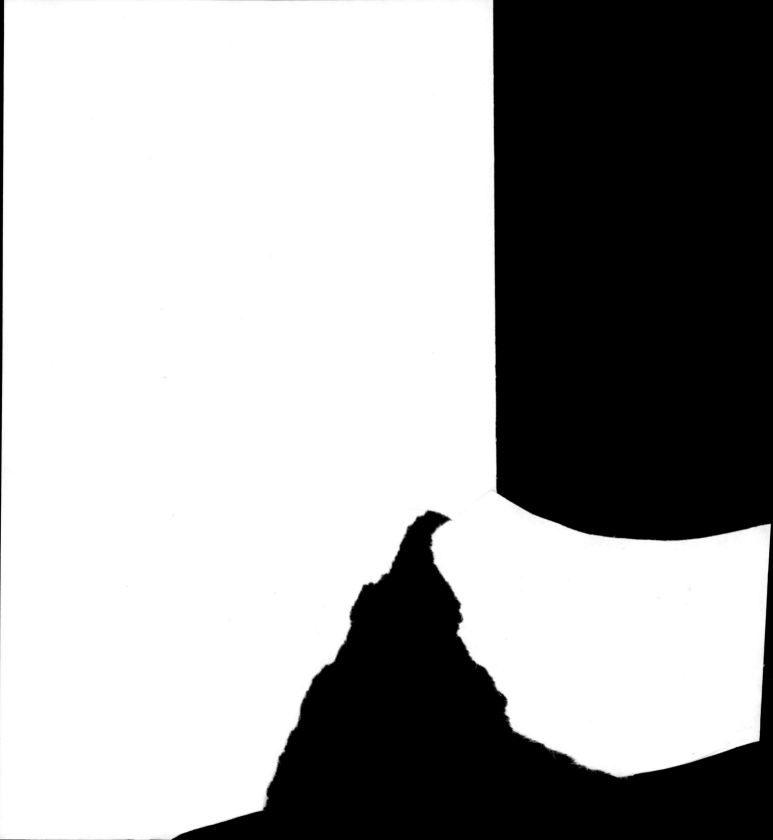

The Narrative Enlarging
A Biography of the Community College—
Nursing Home Partnership Project

Verle Waters, MA, RN

National League for Nursing Press • New York
Pub. No. 14-2681

This book was set in Goudy by Publications Development Company, Crockett, Texas. The editor was Maryan Malone; the designer was Allan Graubard. Clarkwood Corp. was the printer and binder.

Printed in the United States of America

About the Author

Verle Waters, MA, RN, is Dean Emerita, Ohlone College, Fremont, California, and Project Consultant, Community College-Nursing Home Partnership.

Contents

Foreword

Private philanthropy in the United States is a precious resource. The amount of funding available from private resources is minuscule compared to public funding. This limited resource of private funding is best used as venture capital to support the development and testing of social innovations. The challenge to all those entrusted with responsibility for stewardship of these resources is that of assessing the potential of proposed projects to "make a difference"—to leverage positive change that will extend beyond the life of a specific project. The Community College-Nursing Home Partnership project is an outstanding example of how a relatively small investment of private funding resulted in a sweeping change in associate degree nursing education and in building partnerships between two community-based organizations, the community college and nursing homes. As a result of these partnerships, care for the elderly in nursing homes has improved. The ongoing partnerships that have been established will continue to the benefit of both the elders being cared for in nursing home settings and students being educated in associate degree nursing programs throughout the country.

This monograph "tells the story" of this highly successful community college-nursing home partnership. From the initial idea, through the formative stages, to successful implementation, evaluation, and dissemination, the process is described and the lessons learned summarized. This is a story that shows effective leadership in action—at national and local levels—of faculty open to forging into uncharted territory—of nurses and nursing home personnel committed to caring for the elderly and opening their settings for education of students—and of true partnerships at multiple levels—all working together to achieve the goals of the project. I would encourage all who are engaged in providing leadership for change to draw from the rich lessons learned to guide them in their efforts.

Perhaps one of the most important lessons that nurses and nursing educators can learn from this story is the importance of looking beyond the narrow boundaries and "self-interests" of the profession. By joining in a partnership to "improve the health of people," faculty, students, and nursing home personnel joined together in a mission that transcended an internal focus upon nursing and nursing education. The rich experiential world of the nursing home provided a context that stimulated the process of curricular change. The engagement of faculty with nursing home staff to address their learning needs not only enriched the practice domain but was fed back into the curricular change process.

In learning from this experience, it is important to bear in mind that this is a story of partnerships, not the more common experience of outreach or clinical placements of students. While building partnerships requires intensive work to forge true collaboration, the end result is a powerful example of how nurses in practice and nursing educators can become a powerful force for change. Given the current challenges of changing the orientation from a medical care to a health care system, I encourage nurses to explore avenues to build other partnerships that will provide momentum for this needed change in direction.

Helen Grace, PhD, RN
Vice President-Program
W. K. Kellogg Foundation

Preface

This book is about an educational change project. I will try to describe the organization and activities of the project as they relate to its final success. The project, "The Community College-Nursing Home Partnership: Improving Care Through Education," sought to improve the teaching of gerontological nursing and the care of elders in nursing homes. To meet these purposes, the W. K. Kellogg Foundation of Battle Creek, Michigan, provided seven years of funding for a demonstration phase (1986–1990) followed by a dissemination phase (1990–1993). Beginning with only six demonstration sites, the project had an effect which was by all accounts dramatic. By the end of the dissemination period, more than 250 schools of nursing had participated in project-related activities and reported changes in the amount and type of instruction in gerontological nursing, changes which usually included a first-ever clinical placement for senior nursing students in nursing homes. In fact, the success of the project exceeded my own ambitious expectations. In thinking about this, I also realized that I wanted to understand what it was about this particular project that accounted for its influence. Others who carried major responsibility for the project were similarly interested in knowing more about how and why the changes in faculty and curriculum took place, and we believed an analysis of the ingredients of success here might be useful to others planning a similar kind of project for change in and through education. As the project funding period neared termination, we decided to make an anecdotal study of the factors contributing to project success and to share our findings with others—thus, this book.

We hope that this report of our perceptions of how and why the Community College-Nursing Home Project worked will be helpful. There are at least three ways in which it might provide some assistance to nurse educators. First, faculty and administrators in college and service-based educational programs who are planning a grant proposal will find help in developing a structure and modus operandi for meeting project activities. This is not a book about grant writing, or grant finding, but it may be a useful supplement to the many books and articles on that topic in that it explores the significance of internal project structure to external outcomes.

Second, this account of an educational change offers a model for others contemplating revision in programs of study. Planning for changes in the curriculum, an endemic preoccupation among nursing educators, is reaching epidemic proportions in the current climate of health care reform and changing delivery structures. Future registered nurse roles and the preparatory program of study are not at all clear, but there is widespread agreement that the present curriculum with its nearly exclusive focus on nursing roles in the acute care general hospital has serious flaws and deficiencies.

Third, today's teachers with background and special skills in acute care are uncertain about and often resistant to clinical teaching in nonhospital settings. New teaching strategies are necessary for effective learning in nonhospital settings. In our project, faculty who considered themselves acute care specialists took clinical teaching assignments in nursing homes; their stories about how they made the transition and what they learned will be helpful to other teachers who need or want to become teachers in community settings other than the hospital.

The format of the book derives from the objectives established for the project. Chapter 1 describes project origins, general structure, and implementation strategies; four chapters follow, addressing faculty development, nursing home affiliations, community outreach, and evaluation. At the end of the first three chapters there is a summary of "lessons learned" which could serve as a checklist for those who are developing plans for an educational change project or making decisions in the midst of an ongoing project. Finally, in Chapter 6, I summarize the lessons learned about project management, leadership strategies, and educational change.

My purpose is not to present or discuss outcomes of the Community College-Nursing Home Partnership project. Major findings were reported by Dr. Helen Hanson, Project Evaluator, in the project newsletter *Newslink* and elsewhere; selected reports by Dr. Hanson are included in Appendix B. Hanson's role within the project went well beyond outcome evaluation: in Chapter 5, she describes her role and elaborates on evaluation as planning.

The many teachers who brought the idea of this project to life by creating new learning experiences for students in classrooms and nursing homes are the heroines and heros in this enlarging narrative of caring for elders. Many of their best ideas about teaching are presented in two books, a videotape, and several articles written and published earlier by those of us on the project staff. A full listing of publications generated by the project is included as Appendix C.

A report I read more than 20 years ago triggered the idea for this book and has influenced my approach to the topic. Entitled A *Foundation Goes to School* (Nachtigal, 1972), the report analyzed a group of projects funded by the Ford Foundation between 1960 and 1970 to improve public education. The schools that received funding were thought of as "lighthouses," expressing the hope that, as they developed new more effective educational methods, they would, like a beacon, enlighten methods of teaching in the schools around them. The analysis, authorized and published by the Foundation, describes the goals of the funding effort, and examines project effectiveness in relation to "governing structures, operational placement of the projects, selection of the project participants, implementation techniques, project leadership, mobilization of additional resources, community size, grant size, and the timing of grants." Ideas about the design and management of projects intended to bring about a change in educational practices emerge from the analysis and I have attempted to examine our project from a similar perspective.

The Ford Foundation report, A *Foundation Goes to School,* was authored by an analyst not connected with any of the school improvement projects funded by the Foundation. This present book is quite different—it is written by someone who was intimately involved with the Community College-Nursing Home project. Moreover, the ideas and opinions expressed in this text represent the perceptions of a number of people who were intimately associated with the project.

I have used the pronouns "we" and "I" throughout. In Chapter 1, which describes the period of proposal development, the "we" usually means Susan Sherman, Helen Hanson, and myself. In Chapters 2 through 5, the "we" represents the group of 20 to 25 people who carried principal roles for the life of the project. Called "project principals" or "project staff" in this text, the group included the 6 directors of the pilot group nursing programs, a project coordinator from each campus, and other faculty assigned to a project role. The names and educational affiliations of the project principals is found in Appendix E. To remember and describe what we were thinking and doing at various points in the life of the project, I made a thorough review of meeting minutes, project publications, reports, correspondence, and my own notes from 1985 through 1993. During the last months of the project, focused evaluative discussions were held with project staff members and the advisory committee. In addition, to encourage reflective thinking about how the project worked, a survey of project principals, advisory board members, and nursing home partners was conducted in 1993, during the closing months of the project period. The purpose of the survey, as explained in the survey directions, was "to obtain from the key players in The Community College-Nursing Home Partnership Project their perceptions of the project's achievements and what contributed to them." I draw heavily on Helen Hanson's thematic analysis of the survey responses. For readers who might be interested, the survey forms are found in Appendix D.

My account of project activities is more about successes than failures. Although my intent was to discuss the project from the standpoint of what *didn't* work out as well as what did, the fact is I found much more to say about the structures and activities that worked well. I recount some plans and intentions that never happened or fizzled and so were dropped, but those are short stories. When things went well, the story is longer and there is more to tell. There were also conflicts, misunderstandings, hurt feelings, communication errors, and other similarly normal occurrences in human interaction. None persisted, or eroded the open, productive relationships that characterized group interaction. In Chapter 5, we discuss the role that emerged for Helen Hanson as project evaluator; she became something of a sounding board and counselor for upsets that occurred along the way.

For all of us who were actively associated with this project, the experience was extraordinary. It was my last big undertaking at the end of a long career in nursing education, and I brought to it whatever small gains I have made along the way as an educational leader. I think the leadership role is important, and I have discussed it in chapters which follow, but any part which Susan Sherman and I played is far too small to account for the strength and vitality that emerged in this project. A powerful synergy developed in the work of the 20 or so people who carried the burden of the project. We learned from each other, and grew together. It is to all of us that this book is dedicated.

REFERENCES

Nachtigal, P. (1972). *A foundation goes to school: The Ford Foundation comprehensive school improvement program, 1960–1970.* New York: Ford Foundation.

1

Shaping an Idea into a Project Proposal

A project grant proposal begins in the mind as a shapeless notion connected to an uneven assortment of intentions. Some intentions are high-minded; they will be refined and polished into shining purposes. Other intentions, eminently practical, reflect the need for new money and time to achieve desired goals. Tracing the evolution of the ideas that ultimately become a project proposal is difficult if not impossible; memory preserves a few turning points or "aha's," but the details of the deliberations and conversations that helped bring shape and substance to the notion are vague or altogether gone. There are weeks or months of rumination and conversation with those who might be involved. Deliberate discussions with other peers are pursued, raising questions in the discussion that serve as probes for affirmation that the idea is a good one and inviting criticism or a different perspective. Some conversations are guarded so as not to count chickens ahead of hatching, or give away embryos that another might hatch. In time, either the notion begins to take shape and work begins on a proposal, or it fails to take shape and eventually evaporates.

For all of us in nursing education, the last quarter of this century has been a period of growing awareness of the need for improved gerontologic nursing instruction in undergraduate and graduate nursing programs. Along with the marked increase in the numbers of older people, we have seen expectations for gerontological health care and illness services undergo a virtual revolution. Research has dramatically expanded the knowledge base of gerontology and gerontological nursing

1

and medicine. Registered nurse roles have changed to match changes in the larger circumstance, and faculty are challenged to examine the static and cursory treatment of gerontologic nursing topics that lingers in the typical undergraduate program.

Before 1980, nursing education literature about the aged consisted largely of attitude studies describing what nursing students thought and felt about older people, with few articles proposing what or how nursing students should be taught about the care of elderly patients (Burnside, 1985, pp. 121, 127). With the advent of growing popular and professional attention to the burgeoning population of frail and chronically ill older adults, a few nursing authors began urging educators to improve instruction in knowledge of aging and the care of chronically ill older adults (Aiken, 1981; Bahr, 1981; Brower, 1981, 1983, 1985; Gunter & Estes, 1979) and national nursing organizations sponsored conferences and publications urging more attention to the unique nursing needs of older people.

In the mid-1980s, two experienced nurse educators (this author and Susan Sherman, both of whom would assume administrative roles when the project was ultimately realized) sat in a dimly lit corner of a hotel lobby at a national nursing meeting and held the first of a number of conversations about a broad-based project to improve gerontological nursing instruction in the nation's nearly 800 associate degree nursing programs. In the beginning, the conversations were a melange of vague notions, ambitious intentions, and practical considerations. Lacking any coherence at this stage, the discussions leapt back and forth from grand generalizations to detailed notions about day-to-day operations. Now forgotten scenarios were sketched and then abandoned. We were impelled forward by the conviction that the need was clear and the idea and time were right. Both of us were dedicated to community college education in nursing, and shared an ideology about the mission of the community college to respond to changing community needs for health care services. To us the "demographic imperative" contained a clarion call for community college nursing education, and it remained only to deliberate on how that call should be answered.

Drawing on our own experiences with and general knowledge about funded projects, we discussed several wherein educational change had been a major purpose. We dwelt on those that appeared not to have achieved any substantive or lasting effect and speculated on possible reasons for failure. We asked ourselves how a project plan might forestall similar difficulties. We examined positive models as well. I had been a faculty member and then director of one of the pilot programs in Mildred Montag's 1952–1957 eight-site Cooperative Research Project establishing associate degree nursing education, and the design and operation of that project resurfaced in my mind. The more contemporary Robert Wood Johnson (RWJ)-funded Teaching Nursing Home project was an important influence (Schneider, 1984). The RWJ project enabled 11 baccalaureate and graduate schools of nursing to establish clinical teaching affiliations with an equal number of large nursing homes to demonstrate the benefits of university-nursing home affiliations. The focus of the RWJ project prompted us to define a parallel role: We would develop a project to enable affiliations between associate degree nursing programs (of which there were 780 at the time) and small community nursing homes (of which there are some 15,000) scattered throughout rural and urban America. We found it exciting to think of pairing them up. While the academic health science centers in the Teaching Nursing Home project emphasized research and baccalaureate and graduate education, we envisioned a "grass roots" project developing affiliation between nursing homes and the system of nursing education that provides the greatest number of registered nurses. As part of the strategy of effecting curriculum change, we would engage faculty in the development of the nursing home as a clinical placement site for nursing students. The common wisdom among nursing faculty held that the nursing home provided "poor" learning experiences for students, and we understood that any curriculum change that added clinical instruction in nursing home settings would require change in faculty attitudes toward that setting.

DEFINING OUR GOALS

As our discussions continued, a project rationale began to emerge, and the idea of shaping the project to specifically include the nursing home as a place for student learning took on importance. We were influenced by a paragraph from Dr. Robert Butler's report of participation in the Teaching Nursing Home Project:

> *Many efforts have been made to alter the behavior and therefore the attitudes and activities of nursing homes through regulation. Regulations and the enforcement of regulations have not been altogether successful. It is unlikely that education will do the total job either, but it could create important standards and provide pre-service and in-service training*

for those who work within nursing homes by introducing the kinds of dis-
turbing and penetrating questions that students always ask and by stim-
ulating the intellectual curiosity, even passion, that dedicated physicians,
nurses, social workers, and other health professionals are able to provide
in the nursing home setting. (Butler, 1984)

The impetus to provide education for those who work in nursing homes as well as our own students was reinforced by another source of influence: the W.K. Kellogg Foundation, where we intended to seek funding, emphasized the importance of a health services *delivery* component in all project proposals. The idea that had begun amorphously now had focus and structure. In the proposal submitted to the Foundation in 1985, we argued that "nursing potential in the nation's nursing homes could be enhanced through the development by associate degree nursing faculty and students of a teaching-learning mission and environment within the nursing home." "With population and life span data pointing to increasing numbers of the frail and dependent aged," the proposal continued, "anticipatory action on the part of nursing educators is clearly called for. The system of associate degree nursing education, imbedded in the structure of communities across this nation, is well positioned to take on this challenge." (An abridged copy of the project proposal is found in Appendix A.)

The project was envisioned as taking place at several sites in different parts of the country, reasoning that since the purpose of our project would be to demonstrate how something might be done *and* how it could influence others to do the same, the case would be better made if the demonstration were conducted at more than one place. Nursing educators have been known to use a "but we are different" reason for not adopting a recommendation, and that defense is weakened when the recommender can point to a project site with similar program or setting characteristics. Major setting variables can be encompassed in a few selected locations—urban and rural, large and small programs (colleges), inner city and suburban, ethnic minority and majority student populations—and the different regions of the country can be represented. The proposal initiators decided that the right number of demonstration sites for this project was six. It was our intent to choose schools with a history of success, stability, and recognized leadership. The project intentions were ambitious, and we believed chances of approaching them improved if we began in strength. In the Ford Foundation project described in the preface where the aim was to bring about change in public education, project sites were thought of as lighthouses, casting a beacon of change over the schools in their immediate region. The concept captured our intent: We saw demonstration site colleges as developing influence-making networks in their own state and region, and for that reason we intended to select associate degree nursing programs with a reputation for strength and leadership.

THE SHINING PURPOSES

Contemporary writers on organizational effectiveness in both profit and not-for-profit sectors speak of the importance of a clearly articulated mission that inspires as well as guides organizational activities and the role of each person in the organization. Stephen Covey accentuates the importance of shared vision and values in organizations and observes that it takes patience, a long-term perspective, and meaningful involvement to create a clear sense of mission within an organization (Covey, 1991). Two major purposes were first proposed for the project; then after discussion and correspondence with Helen Grace at the W.K. Kellogg Foundation, the purposes were revised and enlarged. The discussions prompted by her suggestions clarified and enlarged our thinking and brought us closer to articulating the vision and values that fueled the project. As stated in the proposal as it was approved by the Foundation, the major purposes were to:

1. Develop nursing potential in nursing homes, through in-service education for staff at all levels, to enhance quality of care being delivered, and to establish active teaching centers for nursing education.
2. Demonstrate and influence the re-direction of associate degree nursing education to encompass active preparation for nursing roles in long-term care organizations as well as acute general hospitals.

An early draft to which Dr. Grace responded had placed the second objective first. As educators, we had somewhat automatically thought first of the educational changes we hoped to initiate with the help of the project. Dr. Grace's suggestion that we reorder the two resulted in a perhaps subtle but ultimately extremely significant change in the way we thought about the project, giving more emphasis to our effect on the nursing home and not just our use of it. Dr. Grace made another suggestion later, in the approval letter from the Foundation: " . . . while the major thrust of your proposal is toward improvement of care in nursing homes, the linkage of community colleges to the broader realm of care of the elderly, both in long-term care facilities as well as those in other community-based settings and homes, is of interest to us. We would trust that as the project develops these linkages might be expanded to extend beyond the nursing component of community colleges to other areas of study and beyond nursing homes to broader based community settings." This notion expanded the scope of the project, and we added a third purpose:

3. Stimulate community college faculty interest and involvement in the field of gerontology and the health care of the aged.

As a result we looked at our venture from a larger perspective, and project staff became engaged in a number of highly successful activities we might not otherwise have thought were within the scope of our project. A full discussion of the activities that extended into the larger community follows in Chapter 4.

SELECTING THE DEMONSTRATION SITES

During the period of time that the proposal was in its final stages of review by the Foundation, we turned our attention to enlisting the participation of four additional associate degree programs. Upon notice of funding, the four additional programs would join the Community College of Philadelphia and Ohlone College in California in carrying out project plans and purposes. The proposal had outlined these criteria to be used in selecting nursing programs to serve as demonstration sites:

1. History of successful relationships with clinical agencies and nursing service personnel.
2. Agreement by the full faculty to participate in and support project activities.
3. Accreditated by the National League for Nursing.
4. Participation as clinical affiliates of 1 to 4 nursing homes.
5. Indication of previous successful effort to include gerontologic nursing content.
6. Institutional commitment to continue project activities once funding period is over.

Following extensive discussion and consultation with others who had wide acquaintance with the associate degree community (e.g., Sylvia Edge at the National League for Nursing and Eula Aiken at the Southern

Regional Education Board), we approached four schools that met established criteria and offered the desired diversity: Shoreline Community College in Seattle, Washington; Triton College in River Grove, Illinois, a Chicago suburb; Valencia Community College in Orlando, Florida; and Weber State University in Ogden, Utah which offered an associate degree nursing program throughout the entire state.

The project was intended to operate on two levels: (1) on an overall level as a national project (at some point we began calling it the "umbrella project"), and (2) as six locally based projects. The six locally based projects would each demonstrate a way to meet the national purposes and objectives set forth by the umbrella project. Such a structure is not so much contradictory as an exercise in counterpoise. Questions came up throughout the life of the grant that tested the balance between centralization and decentralization, between similarity and diversity, between conformity and autonomy.

A basic question arose about budget control. Old adages about the linkage of purse and power tempt one to be of the opinion that without control of the budget, one lacks control of activities and outcomes. I had been disabused of that shiboleth some years earlier when I initiated a two-college collaborative project in California. I had assumed that, because the administrative leadership of the project would be located at Ohlone College, full budget management, including receiving and disbursing of all grant funds, should also be located at Ohlone. Allan Frawley, Ohlone Business Manager, raised questions leading to a more thoughtful examination of the issues of budget control. He expressed great reluctance to assuming fiscal responsibility for the reliability and credibility of accounting practices in another business office, a responsibility he saw as a necessary consequence if Ohlone became the sole grantee and recipient of funds. He offered the opinion that the business manager at each participating institution should maintain fiscal accountability to the granting agency, and that the project administrator should find other ways to influence outcome accountability. At his urging, I revised the project structure, defining the project as a unified undertaking with leadership the designated responsibility of Ohlone College. The two participating colleges in that earlier project wrote a separate proposal for funding, but they were submitted together as a package.

With the earlier experience in mind, the community college-nursing home partnership project proposal was jointly submitted by Ohlone College and the Community College of Philadelphia with two separate budget requests. Administrative responsibilities and administrative support services for the national effort were divided between the two institutions and tied to specific functions itemized in the budget requests. I was designated Project Administrator of the national "umbrella" project. The local demonstration project to be carried out by Ohlone College was also under my general direction, but a full-time project director and secretarial assistance was provided for in the Ohlone budget. At Community College of Philadelphia, Susan Sherman was both assistant director for the national project and responsible for the CCP demonstration project. An Administrative Assistant for the national project was located at CCP, assuming responsibility for communication activities, including managing the newsletter, planning meetings, and serving as a source and clearing house for project information.

The intended selection of four additional participating colleges was also outlined in the initial proposal. A budget "template" for the four colleges to follow was included in the original proposal, setting a common total budget figure for each site and identifying major expenditure categories. In addition to budget lines for personnel, equipment, and other expenses associated with carrying out project activities at the particular site, the sample budget included dollar support for attendance at national staff meetings, consultation visits from the project evaluator or project administrators, and other activities we thought might be important to develop coherence within the national effort, to minimize fragmentation, and avoid isolation. Decisions about the allocation of funds between the national and local budgets was made with these factors in mind. We explored the consequences of placing an item in national or local budgets in terms of productivity and intergroup relationships. The decisions that Susan Sherman and I made about budget categories that fell into the national budget and those that fell into the local, and the development of a common budget for the four added sites represented our best effort at striking a balance between centralization as a national project and local autonomy as six demonstration projects. The four new proposals were completed approximately one year after CCP and Ohlone were first funded and the total project concept approved by the Foundation. They were submitted as a package with a cover letter from me as project administrator.

ONE DESTINATION, SIX PATHWAYS

A general definition of the relationship between the umbrella project and the individual sites was established in the project proposal, but answers to many specific questions about demonstration site autonomy and overall project management were worked out as we went along. A basic tenet of the relationship was that the major purposes and the objectives approved by the Foundation for the umbrella project would also be the purposes and objectives for each demonstration site. Each site would determine the activities and operations which would meet those purposes and objectives in their community. In the separate project proposals, developed by nursing faculty at each site, methods and activities to achieve the common objectives were unique to that campus. Each of the four new sites had copies of the Ohlone and Community College of Philadelphia proposals; Susan Sherman and I provided consultation as requested and reviewed drafts of proposals when asked. (Ms. Sherman worked with the Illinois and Florida colleges and I with Washington State and Utah.) We saw a risk of fragmentation if activities at demonstration sites went far afield, but on the other hand neither Susan Sherman nor I wanted to tell schools what they should do or even be the judge of whether an activity or direction taken up by a particular school was on or off target. There was a period of uncertainty among demonstration sites as to whether they were doing "the right thing." There were "assignments" of a sort for activities that were part of the national or umbrella project: preparing for the national "Blueprints" conference (described in Chapter 3); writing articles for *Newslink*, the project newsletter; and participating in the content analysis that followed the DACUM study. This is described briefly in Chapter 3 and more fully in *Teaching Gerontology* (Waters, 1991, pp. 74–77). These activities provided some structure and put faculty in each school in the position of working with faculty of other schools while they were shaping plans for their own project. While we cannot be certain of the reasons for the unity of spirit and purpose that emerged among project principals and contributed to project effectiveness, we believe that some balance between too much and too little central control was struck. As project leader, Waters saw that our course lay between Scylla and Charybdis: lack of direction would lead to diffusion and fragmentation; heavy-handed direction could lead to subversion or apathy. The course steadied with the enlarging discussions among members of this new work group. Monitoring and supervision came from the group itself rather than from Sherman and Waters. As a deliberate leadership strategy, comparisons and competition between sites were actively discouraged. Group meetings were conducted in such a way as to encourage noncompetitive communication and open sharing of ideas, achievements, questions, and problems, and to elicit honest feedback from each other along with strong expressions of support. We had said in the proposal, "The project administrative structure is designed to assure supervision of each demonstration site while providing for strong communication links between and among all projects. . . . Extensive sharing of information about project participants will yield an account of project experiences which will be of considerable use in realizing the two overall purposes of this ambitious project." There are references in later chapters to examples of the extensive sharing, and the use, modification, and elaboration of one another's work.

PLANNING FOR MEANING-MAKING MEETINGS

I carried into the plans for project activities a conviction that a principal, if covert, purpose in every educational change project is the intent to create new professional and personal growth experiences for all who are drawn into the work of the project. There was a missionary touch to this conviction: a sense that associate degree educators, for a number of reasons, are minimally engaged in professional and career development activities, and that a grant-supported project should seek what it can do for the growth of the faculty. The business world of the nineties has added a phrase to the language which captures the concept: today's business leaders are entreated to create "learning organizations" (Wick & Leon, 1993a).

> By consistently stretching the abilities of those who work for them, learning leaders create a dynamic environment that not only places a high value on innovation and knowledge but generates the energy needed to move the organization from contemplation to action . . . creating a learning organization that continually improves by rapidly creating and refining the capabilities needed for future success. (Wick & Leon, 1993b, p. 43.)

While this definition of a learning organization followed our planning period by some years, it describes our point of view. We discussed the location, interval, and purposes of meetings for the project staff from all sites from an educative perspective. At each site, the ADN program director was the project director, and in addition one or two faculty members were wholly or partially supported by grant funds and called "coordinator," or at Shoreline College, "facilitator." These became the core group of "project staff." I requested that substitutes not be sent to the staff meetings; a changing cast of characters would mitigate the intent to create a cohesive, beneficial group.

Once the project was underway, national meetings were taken very seriously, with discussion and detailed planning of agendas and instructions to participants about preparing for the meeting (often including a written summary or report). From the beginning, Helen Hanson, project evaluator, joined Susan Sherman and I in planning meetings. At her suggestion, agenda topics were usually phrased as questions. Meetings had what might be called "process goals" as well as intended outcomes. Follow-up activities after the meeting, including distribution of minutes and other written materials, were planned with similar attention to purpose.

The proposal specified two total staff meetings in the first year of project activities, the first of which was held in March after selection and agreement to participate from the four added sites but before full development of the four additional site proposals. This first meeting provided an opportunity to discuss as a group the purposes and objectives of the project. Most of the program directors knew each other, but faculty members who had been chosen or volunteered to be affiliated with the project were meeting each other for the first time as well as exploring for the first time the purposes and activities outlined in the proposal. One by one and objective by objective, representatives from the six schools were invited to think aloud about what might be done in their college and community to achieve each objective. Minutes from that March 1986 meeting reveal a rich array of possible courses of action. Ideas were discussed, but not weighed; it was important that, at this stage, we not get attached to the outcomes. This first meeting roamed widely over the purpose and overall intent and the inspiring fit between the challenge posed in the project and the strengths of associate degree nursing. Hanson was present, facilitating discussion, and introducing the group to the development of evaluation strategies as an integral part of action plans. (See Chapter 5, Evaluation as Planning.) In summative evaluation discussions held with project staff in 1993, it was said that the first meeting set a pattern that influenced interaction with each other for the length of the project period. As one person expressed it, "the project evolved, and was continually re-formed." At the heart of this is a pattern of communication that is leader-initiated but not "led" in the conventional sense. Project staff at each of the sites were encouraged to engage their respective faculties in exploring how the goals might best be met at their site, and, moreover, they were encouraged to consult with each other. It may be that early frustration and uncertainty along with a strong desire to "do it right" encouraged them to turn to each other. At any rate, they did quickly move into a pattern of frequent exchanges among the staff of the six sites. With every meeting or telephone conversation of two or more of the project principals, the stories joined, and the narrative took shape.

ADVISORY COMMITTEES

An important component in the general design of the project was a national advisory committee. The draft proposal submitted to Helen Grace for critique and suggestions stated that the national advisory committee would "review project goals and dilemmas (as they develop) and provide direction." We included in the proposal a list of persons "under consideration" as advisory committee members, most of them nurse specialists in the area of gerontologic nursing. Once again Dr. Grace broadened our outlook. She encouraged us to re-think our conception of roles and membership on the advisory committee and to seek the participation of principals in related disciplines who would become advocates and spokespersons for the project as well as provide advice regarding project direction and dilemmas. With that in mind, we instituted an advisory board with strong representation from the nursing home industry and other health disciplines and organizations. It was an important change, one that we appreciated a number of times when advisory committee members opened doors that might have been closed and spoke from platforms we could not have mounted. Advisory board meetings were held once a year—a deadening interval if there are no intervening contacts. We watched for opportunities to send mail that would keep board members informed and interested; we watched for opportunities, too, to make telephone contacts on a specific topic with a board member to whom the topic would be relevant. Agendas for the annual meetings of the advisory board were carefully planned and structured to alternate listening to reports or presentations with discussion periods which focused on committee member input. Discussion periods were structured around issues and questions that were "real"; that is, the answers or suggestions were important to the project, and they were about subjects the advisory committee had understanding and insight about. While not every person named in the two advisory boards became an active participant in the project, the greater number did. In 1990 at the end of the demonstration project, the board was reconstituted, with some carry-over.

At the six demonstration sites, a variety of local committees were formed that served an advisory function. At some sites, a new advisory committee for the project was appointed; at another the existing program advisory committee was enlarged to include representatives from nursing homes and long term care organizations. On some campuses, task forces were convened to provide assistance with specific aspects of the project, such as staff development in nursing homes. At all six sites, people and community organizations new to affiliation with collegiate nursing education came to the campuses, invited for the first time to participate in discussions about the curriculum and student learning. Committee members included gerontologists from other disciplines, nursing home administrators, directors of nursing, and staff developers, and geriatric nursing specialists, and other community leaders in advancing the welfare of elders. As nursing educators, we have a long tradition of looking only to the acute care hospitals when we speak of nursing service, and the development of advisory and task groups to work with us on the new project provided the first of many opportunities to see how narrowly we had before that day defined "nursing service community." We found there were many beyond the walls of the acute care hospital that cared about our students and the education they receive.

ADMINISTRATIVE STRUCTURE

From 1986 to 1990, during the demonstration phase, overall project administration was located at Ohlone College in California, but a number of administrative functions, including management of the logistics of advisory board and staff meetings was at the Community College of Philadelphia. A full-time administrative assistant for the project was located at CCP. We found no serious problems with this arrangement; the telephone, the fax machine, Federal Express (now, in the 1990s, E-mail would be a likely addition), and airplane tickets made full communication possible. With the second phase of funding for the dissemination period, 1990–1993, the national office shifted completely to the Community College of Philadelphia and Susan Sherman became project administrator. I retired my academic position at Ohlone College and continued to work with the community college-nursing home project in a consultant role (with designated responsibilities and activities spelled out in the dissemination project proposal). Helen Hanson continued her expanded evaluator role into the dissemination phase of the project.

LESSONS LEARNED

Based on our experiences, we suggest the following in bringing a project into being, getting it organized, and getting started:

1. Think about the beliefs, values, and passions behind your intentions. You want to be able to give voice to them so that you have the words which will inspire others and encourage them to commit whole heartedly to making the project work.

2. Talk a lot about your proposed project to the smartest people you know. Let your ideas roam wild and free at first, moving back and forth between your ideals and practicality. Look for connections between your fondest dreams and stubborn reality.

3. Get as much information as you can about projects that held any similarity to yours. What worked well? What didn't?

4. Learn as much as you can about your intended funding source. What are they funding? What do they say are their priorities? Your intentions and theirs should be the same.

5. Try to involve the people who will be carrying out the project early and continuously in development of the project. Engage in brainstorming sessions. Find and share things to read—articles, news stories, anything—that sharpens the issues the project will address, describes how others are approaching the problem, or illuminates the topic in some way. Ask key persons to draft parts of the proposal.

6. Invite comment from your funding source as your proposal shapes up.

7. If you are the project leader, think realistically about your time. How much time will be left for the project after you meet the demands of your ongoing responsibilities to the organization? Being a good leader takes time. How can the staffing structure you plan for the new project assure you the time you will need? (Hint: Be creative.)

8. As you get underway, try to be clear and articulate about your vision and intentions, and give specific day-to-day activities time to evolve as project principals begin to work together. To the extent possible, let specifics emerge from discussions with the key players. Take time. You want everyone associated with the project to embrace as their own the vision and values that fuel the project's purposes.

REFERENCES

Aiken, L. (1981, February). Nursing priorities for the 1980s in hospitals and nursing homes. *American Journal of Nursing, 324–330.*

Bahr, Sr. R. T. (1981). Overview of gerontological nursing. In M.O. Hogstel (Ed.), *Nursing care of the older adult.* New York: John Wiley.

Brower, H. T. (1981). Teaching gerontological nursing in Florida: Where do we stand? *Nursing and Health Care, 10,* 543–547.

Brower, H. T. (1983). The nursing curriculum for long-term institutional care. In *Creating a career choice for nurses: Long-term care.* (pp. 45–64). New York: The National League for Nursing Press.

Brower, H. T. (1985). Knowledge competencies in gerontological nursing. In *Overcoming the bias of ageism in long-term care.* (pp. 55–82). New York: The National League for Nursing Press.

Burnside, I. (1985). Gerontological nursing research: 1975–1984. In *Overcoming the bias of ageism in long-term care.* (pp. 121, 127). New York: The National League for Nursing Press.

Butler, R. N. (1984). Mount Sinai school of medicine. In E. L. Schneider (Ed.), *The teaching nursing home.* (p. 100). New York: Raven Press.

Covey, S. R. (1991). *Principle-centered leadership.* (pp. 165, 184). New York: Simon & Shuster.

Gunter, L. M., & Estes, C. A. (1979). *Education for gerontic nursing.* New York: Springer.

Schneider, E. L. (Ed.) (1984). *The teaching nursing home.* New York: Raven Press.

Waters, V. (Ed.) (1991). *Teaching gerontology.* New York: National League for Nursing Press.

Wick, C. W., & Leon, L. S. (1993a). *The learning edge: How smart managers and smart companies stay ahead.* New York: McGraw-Hill.

Wick, C. W., & Leon, L. S. (1993b). 11 ways to turn your staff into lifelong learners. *Executive Female,* Mar/Apr 1993, 44–48.

2

Faculty and Staff Development: The Gateway to Curriculum Change

FACULTY DEVELOPMENT FIRST

We would learn, as project activities got underway, how deeply resistant to the idea of the project some of our own faculty, along with others in associate degree nursing, were. Fears were expressed that the project would become merely the first downward step on a slippery slope ending in the relegation of associate degree nursing graduates to jobs in nursing homes, or that student applicants would fail to appear once they learned that the nursing home was part of clinical education, or that graduates would begin failing the N-CLEX exam because time spent on gerontology content would deprive them of more essential learning, or that in allying ADN programs with nursing homes, we gave "entry-into-practice" advocates an opportunity to formalize invidious distinctions between AD and BS graduates. (The biases imbedded in each of these troubled predictions might be funny if not so egregious.)

These attitudes were hardly a surprise, given the historical background of the nursing home, its isolation from academic programs, and the well-known work preferences of nurses and others in health care for acute settings over chronic, for the young over the old, and for cure over care. But surprising or not, negative attitudes and resistance on the part of the teaching faculty posed a formidable challenge to the promises made in the grant proposal. We knew that faculty reeducation was a crucial first step for any substantive and lasting change in the curriculum and the learning experiences provided for the students (Hanson & Waters, 1991).

Educational research does not shed much light on what motivates faculty to change or improve their teaching. The question has proved to be a difficult one to answer, or is answered by: "It depends"—on the type of educational institution, on the nature of the student population, and on the faculty person her or himself. A survey of educational research that studied methods of motivating teachers to change found two general approaches described: giving rewards, and specifying preparation (Stark & Mets, 1988). Reward solutions include any change in work assignment, organizational structure, or recognition that induces faculty members to change or improve their teaching. Time, money, or other benefits and resources are allocated to reward desired changes or improvements in teaching performance. Preparation solutions, on the other hand, take the form of pressure to change educational requirements for becoming a teacher or for continuing to teach (that is, for maintaining teaching credentials).

Each of our six demonstration colleges developed its own plan for educating and influencing the attitudes of the teaching faculty, and both reward and preparation solutions were employed. No effort was made to create a common approach to faculty development; each campus was encouraged to plan development activities that best suited its faculty, and to call on one another as desired to discuss and share ideas and approaches. Every campus followed a different course of action in attempting to educate faculty and to influence their thinking about the teaching of gerontological nursing and the nursing home. While each site felt satisfied at the end of the project period that faculty development goals had been met, there were differences in the amount of time it took for each of the six faculties to become actively engaged in project activities, to make curriculum changes in the teaching of gerontology, and to demonstrate support for the project goals and purposes. We can only speculate on the possible relationship between methods used to motivate faculty to change and the time it took for actual curriculum changes to be made, but we include some observations about relative effectiveness of the varied approaches later in this chapter when development activities on each of the campuses are described.

The project proposal stated that faculty development would be a necessary means to achieving project outcomes, and specified an immediate budget for faculty development activities. We knew that change in the way our faculties looked at gerontological nursing and nursing homes was critical. Evidence that attitudes were changing and interest growing began to accumulate, earlier on some campuses than others, but eventually at all of them. At the close of the project, when asked what they felt contributed to the success of the project, project principals cited faculty development more often than any other factor. Responses included these comments:

- The focus on faculty development FIRST gave faculty confidence necessary to move forward.
- The fact that the grant provided funds "up front" for educating faculty before they had to produce had a positive effect on faculty.
- Knowledge was the key factor; it was critical in helping us get over the hump.
- Faculty development was the first building block to curriculum revision.

We have made the point in Chapter 1 that we deliberately emphasized the importance of faculty development in national staff meetings, and that national meetings themselves were planned and conducted as sessions in which participants would have the opportunity to expand their skills and understanding. Staff meetings were planned and conducted so as to create an atmosphere of support and challenge. It was our intention to develop a team and to foster relationships among the team members that would permit them to turn to each other for advice and support.

Writers in organizational effectiveness speak of a "shared vision of the mission of the organization" (Covey, 1991, p.184). Put another way, organizational values are seen as important to success, and the organizational leader initiates and maintains a process of ongoing values clarification (Vaill, 1989, p.59). We were convinced that no curriculum change (other than on paper) could occur without changing values, interests, and the knowledge base of faculty. First, we recognized that in asking faculty to agree to more classroom and clinical time for gerontological nursing, we were asking them to embrace a subject weighted with negative social and professional attitudes, stereotypes, and biases. We were asking them to agree to the clinical placement of senior students in nursing homes, a setting seen by most faculty as below par in standards of care and opportunities for student learning, and we were asking a group of faculty educated as and hired because they were acute care specialists to care about improving instruction in long-term care nursing at a time when the ever more high-tech hospital was escalating the demand for new graduate proficiency in acute care. (Associate degree programs have since their inception geared instruction to the work of the registered nurse in a general acute-care hospital, and so have traditionally employed teachers with established interest and skill in acute-care nursing. It is true, of course, that patients in acute general hospitals include people who are old and considered "geriatric," but most nurses would agree that the ethos of nursing practice in the acute care hospital directed more attention to the illness care of the patient than to age-related variables.)

EACH SITE TOOK A
DIFFERENT APPROACH

The stage was set for faculty development activities within our project at the first meeting (1986) of all project staff. The question of how to engage faculty in the new project was discussed at length. The goal was for every member of the faculty to learn more about gerontological nursing, and to value it as a component of the basic curriculum. Not everyone on the faculty would be teaching gerontological nursing, but it would be important for lasting program changes to have all faculty in support.

At Valencia college, the dean and the nursing department chairperson promptly initiated a series of off-campus retreats to engage the full faculty in learning about aging and nursing practice in geriatric settings. The faculty member who served as project coordinator observed that the dean, in scheduling the workshops immediately upon funding, sent the message that "we're all in this together; we're starting together and we want to move together." While this approach worked very well at Valencia, it might not have at all schools. The project coordinator felt that "a lot depended on the way it was presented by the dean and department chair. It was more of a socialization than a mandate." Led by local experts in gerontology and gerontologic nursing, the workshops included between-term clinical and field assignments which required each faculty member (including the dean, chairperson, and project coordinator) to interact with an aging client, record the interaction, and discuss the experience with fellow-faculty.

Quite a different approach to faculty development and participation in project activities, although one that was also effective, developed at Shoreline College. The program director and project staff (two members of the faculty) offered the faculty two levels of involvement. The purpose was to offer a choice as to the level of involvement in project activities, intending that everyone would choose one or another of the two categories, and that no one would choose to have *no* part in the new project. The categories were as follows:

1. Category One: (a) work on curriculum committee or team which identifies content; (b) teach with geriatric content included, and (c) attend at least one educational event to increase gerontological base.
2. Category Two: (a) all category one activities plus (b) take additional course(s), and (c) teach a continuing education course, or work with outside person to develop course, or work with a registered nurse staff and nursing home as a consultant.

Each faculty member was asked to respond in writing and work out an individual plan with project facilitators and the program director.

At the Community College of Philadelphia, a faculty member who had a gerontological nursing and nursing home background became a one-woman blitz of fact sheets (which she wrote) on various gerontological nursing topics and photocopies of articles and reports, all of which swelled faculty mailboxes. By the time the fact sheets had reached the end of their usefulness (about two years), three faculty members who were known as the risk-takers and generally trusted by the faculty to try new ideas had become interested in the project. They provided enthusiastic leadership until the end of the project.

The quick adoption of the use of fact sheets at other demonstration sights is an early example of the sharing of ideas and practices which marked inter-school relationships. At Valencia College, fact sheets were used for student instruction as well as faculty growth. (See further discussion of the nature and use of fact sheets in *Teaching Gerontology* (Waters, 1991).)

Ohlone faculty began to engage with the project cautiously. At the time of funding, they felt fully scheduled, noting that a major curriculum revision was underway. To begin, a portion of the regular Monday afternoon faculty meeting was allocated once a month to project purposes. With skillful programming by the project coordinator, interest and involvement grew steadily. Later in this chapter, in the discussion on curriculum change, we will note that the fact that the Ohlone faculty were in the midst of a major revision made the addition of a new course with a nursing home clinical affiliation easier than it was in other sites.

At Weber State University, a nearby Geriatric Education Center was then offering a program of study and certification in gerontology for health professionals. Project leaders on that campus (program director

and project coordinator) announced a plan to support and give a financial reward to faculty who enrolled in and successfully completed the certification course. A number of nursing faculty responded to the offer. Of
those who took the courses and enjoyed the financial award, some continued a working interest in the project and some did not.

Full faculty engagement in the grant and its activities was slow to come
at Weber, and in the opinion of the project staff members, began to
change late in the life of the project only when the members of the nursing faculty seen by others as powerful became involved. At Triton College,
also, political factors in the college community may have distracted faculty and delayed full project endorsement until later in the life of the project, when tenured faculty became more supportive. Our experience
confirmed the practicality of the maxim that if you want to bring about
a change in the curriculum, coopt the faculty oligarchy. A recorded
discussion in a focus group quotes a faculty member in a program where
significant change had occurred as saying to the person who had spear-
headed changes, "I was the one who was most against it. I went in (to
teach a clinical group in the nursing home) because you were a trusted
member of our faculty and I trusted you and _____(department
chair) said that we needed to do this, and so I said, "Well I guess that I
have to do this but there was no other reason. I am really being very honest about it. To my utter surprise it was a wonderful experience."

Observing and working with extramurally funded change projects prior
to writing the proposal for this project had persuaded this author that
project success might depend on the availability of a full-time, respected,
tenured member of the faculty for the project coordinator role. At the
conclusion of the project years, I now believe that although it is desirable
to have a change project led by a "core" faculty member, given other conditions, successful change can be coordinated by an "outsider." At three
of the demonstration sites, an outside person was recruited: Weber appointed a part-time faculty member as project coordinator and Triton and
Ohlone appointed coordinators who were new to the faculty. On these
three campuses, no tenured faculty were available for the position. Difficulties can be anticipated when someone who is not part of the established faculty culture comes in to carry out the work of a project of
educational change. If the change is at all unpopular, as ours certainly
was, the outsider hired with a fixed-term appointment faces often daunting challenges. With three of our demonstration sites appointing respected tenured faculty to the coordinator role and three appointing
newcomers, it would be satisfying to have observed clear differences in
the curriculum change that was achieved. No such differences appeared,

however. We have concluded that other factors are important, perhaps equally important to project success:

1. All three of the outsiders who came in to coordinate the project were academically qualified, clinically competent, energetic women with strong "people skills."

2. All three remained in their positions for the full life of the project. The analysis of the Ford Foundation educational change projects described in the preface found a distinct relationship between the effectiveness and productivity of a project and tenure in project leadership.

3. The length of the project itself was a factor in bringing about curriculum change at every site, according to the coordinators. They believe that the extended period of the grant, 3 years in demonstration activities and 3 years in dissemination (with the advance year for planning, Ohlone and CCP were funded for a total of 7 years), provided the time that it took for some faculty to make changes in thought and action consistent with the intention of the project.

   "Some faculty who've seen projects come and go simply held back. When they saw this one was there to stay for awhile, they came on board."

   "The fact that the Foundation gave us more money for the dissemination phase converted the hold-outs. Now they were convinced this must really be an important project."

As noted in Chapter 1, a significant part of faculty development was the intentional structure given to national staff meetings. A special meeting was held in Orlando, Florida, in October 1988 to bring together a number of faculty from each campus to share with each other "current and future activities planned for project sites to accomplish project goals." Pairs of faculty from each demonstration site prepared short workshop sessions; 12 90-minute workshops were offered in the 2-day meeting. Among the workshop titles, the following illustrate the topics that were discussed:

- The Right Stuff: Evolving Partnerships
- Curriculum "How Tos"
- Faculty Development at Valencia

- Building Self-Esteem of Nursing Home Staff
- Dare to be Different: Focus on the Clinical Environment
- The Geriatric Clinical Experience: Wellness and Illness

Beneficial outcomes of this early national meeting were lasting. Faculty from each campus saw themselves and their program as part of a national project as well as a local one. Following this meeting, telephone contact between campuses occurred frequently, and print materials were shared regularly. In the words of one participant,

> It was self-esteem building for faculty to become a resource for other faculty.

National meetings were used to encourage project principals in the development of new skills, new perspectives, and wider involvement in professional and community activities. Prior to becoming a coordinator or facilitator for the new project, each of these staff members had held teaching positions. They had little or no previous experience speaking outside of the classroom or writing for publication. We began early encouraging all of us who worked with the project to offer to speak at local and regional professional meetings, to submit papers for conference presentation, to write articles for publication in nursing home industry journals as well as nursing journals, and in all ways to pursue opportunities to talk about the project to other nurse educators, to the nursing home community, and others in the larger field of gerontology. News articles, speeches, poster ideas, and all such materials were shared among project staff at all sites. Teams of two or three, often from different campuses, became repeat performers at professional and trade association meetings. In consequence, public speaking skills were developed, writing skills improved, confidence and articulateness grew.

At the beginning of the dissemination phase of the project, a special workshop was developed to help with the expanded role now called for. With the end of the demonstration period and the new purpose of selling the idea and the work of the project to other faculties and nursing homes in their geographic region, project faculty and coordinators expressed a need for training in the skills of consultation and organizational development. A team of experts in these fields was engaged, and an experiential workshop held in Denver in 1990. The workshop leaders used a videotape to open the first session which the group responded to enthusiastically, and later used to good effect with other faculty groups who were working to improve the teaching of gerontological nursing (Charthouse International Learning Corporation, 1989).

While curriculum change as a project goal was being worked on from the beginning, the implementation of changes in the curriculums of the six demonstration sites proceeded on a different timetable for each. At Ohlone College a major revision of curriculum design and structure was underway at the time the project was funded, and it was possible to insert a new gerontological nursing course in the fourth semester with clinical placement in the nursing home. By faculty consent the courses-and-hours slate had been wiped clean, so to speak, and time allocation in all subject areas had to be defended anew. The case for time allocation to a gerontological nursing course with a nursing home clinical placement was accepted with some reluctance but not with dissent because no faculty member or teaching team could feel that they were giving up time from their teaching domain. On the other campuses time for additional classroom and clinical instruction in gerontological nursing during the last year of the student's program had to be negotiated in programs already intense. At Shoreline, the curriculum time allocated to the teaching of management skills was expanded, gerontologic content added, and the nursing home used as a practice site for the management role in nursing. Valencia college inserted an elective in the nursing home and permitted only honors students to enroll, thus creating a demand from all students for such an experience. CCP divided an existing adult medical-surgical nursing course and allocated half of the clinical time to the nursing home. Weber and Triton created popular elective courses which on their merit earned a place in the required curriculum.

Creating space in a crowded curriculum for a new topic is essentially a political process. Once space is bargained for, the question of how to use the time still must be answered. We have discussed elsewhere the content domain in gerontological nursing (Waters, 1991, pp. 35–54) and the steps we followed in identifying what students would learn about nursing practice in nursing homes. (See the discussion of the DACUM analysis which follows in Chapter 3.)

There are many barriers and stumbling blocks in the road to making a substantive change in the nursing curriculum. Our experience tells us that with good leadership, judicious help, and time, a faculty will find ways of dealing with the barriers and blocks. Our experience also tells us that once faculty initiates change, gerontologic nursing and the nursing home sell themselves. In the words of a faculty member:

*Incorporation of geri content into the curriculum has proven its worth
and is there to stay.*

LESSONS LEARNED ABOUT
FACULTY DEVELOPMENT

Sifting through the final survey forms, and listening to project principals as
they summed up what they learned about faculty development, we can make
a list of what might be called tips or potentially useful ideas about faculty
development as a necessary means to any intended educational change.

1. Involve all faculty in planning the faculty development activities.

2. Identify a "cheerleader" and give her or him time to coordinate
   planning, to consult widely, and recruit supporters, and to look
   for, photocopy, and route pertinent materials.

3. Bring in experts (or use experts on your faculty) to conduct workshops or study sessions. Pick workshop leaders who you know will
   be appealing role models for the desired change.

4. Check out resources that might be available at nearby universities, health service organizations, or professional associations.
   Guest experts who hold stature in the community or the profession will increase faculty respect for the intended change.

5. Hold workshops and study sessions on the campus or in other really convenient locations, at times convenient for faculty.

6. Provide continuing, vigilant leadership. Maintain the vision, keep
   people on target, encourage and validate success, help faculty see
   value and purpose in their work.

7. As a leader, communicate the expectation that everyone will participate in some fashion.

8. Find or allocate—from somewhere—time and money resources to
   fuel the change. Attaching time and money resources to faculty
   development has both symbolic and real importance.

9. Focus on the faculty recognized as informal leaders. Unless the
   oligarchy is supportive of, or at least not opposed to the intended
   changes, they are not likely to occur.

10. Bring out in the open as honest concerns what you know to be threatened self-interests: teaching "favorite" content, overwork, status associated with particular assignments, choice clinical settings, and so on.

11. Negotiate with people to take on a new assignment in long-term care on a trial basis. (Offer incentives and trade-offs. Make a genuine offer to discontinue if they wish after the trial period.) In our project those who agreed to take on a teaching assignment in the nursing home (and they included faculty from virtually every specialty), the educational experience of the trial period was intense and effective. By their own accounts, attitudes toward nursing and teaching practices changed substantially.

12. Stay flexible. Expect the unexpected, and don't get attached to the outcomes in faculty development.

REFERENCES

Charthouse International Learning Corporation, Producer (1989). *The Business of Paradigms.* (A 38-minute videotape.) Burnsville, MN: Charthouse International Learning Corporation.

Covey, S. R. (1991). *Principle-centered leadership.* New York: Simon & Schuster.

Hanson, H. A., & Waters, V. (1991). The sequence of curriculum change in gerontology: Faculty first. *Nursing and Health Care, 12,* 516–519.

Stark, J. S., & Mets, L. A. (Eds.) (1988). *Improving teaching and learning through research.* San Francisco: Jossey-Bass.

Vaill, P. B. (1989). *Managing as a performing art.* San Francisco: Jossey-Bass.

Waters, V. (Ed.) (1991). *Teaching gerontology.* New York: National League for Nursing Press.

3

The Nursing Home:
Creating a New Setting for Learning

The centerpiece of the project, as its title suggests, was the development of a partnership between the nursing school and nursing homes. The proposal predicted that the faculty at each demonstration site would establish educational partnerships with 1 to 4 nursing homes, with the expectation that long-term, stable relationships between each nursing program and specified nursing homes would develop. The terms "partnership" and "collaboration" were an integral part of our discussions, and throughout the life of the project staff members spoke of "partner nursing homes" and "nursing home partners." Differences emerged, however, and while some partnerships developed into strong and stable educational affiliations, others did not. By the end of the first year, we began to see how quickly change can sweep through a nursing home, bringing staff replacements, program shifts, and resource reallocation. Sometimes, because of the changes, educational placement of students was terminated in that nursing home. The question of exactly what the elements of a successful partnership were became more interesting. Following one advisory board discussion, Sharon Simpson, a member, and Andrea Mengel of the Community College of Philadelphia faculty undertook a study to answer that question. Using questionnaires and a three-round Delphi technique, Mengel and coworkers identified the values and opinions of faculty and nursing home personnel engaged in the development of partnerships. Their findings, discussed in the last section of this chapter, identify

29

essential factors in a successful community college-nursing home partnership (Mengel, Simson, Sherman, & Waters, 1991). The body of research literature on factors which influence successful collaboration was recently reviewed and summarized (Mattessich & Monsey, 1992), reflecting the growing interest in and importance of collaborative arrangements between human service, government, and community organizations. In the final section of this chapter, we will review the criteria for a successful collaborative relationship identified by Mattessich and Monsey and the Mengel study, and examine the extent to which community college-nursing home partnerships satisfy those criteria. But first we offer a narrative account of the activities developed by project staff for the purpose of establishing and maintaining educational partnerships with nursing homes.

ASSESSING EDUCATIONAL NEEDS: THE STARTING POINT FOR STAFF DEVELOPMENT

At the first meeting of project principals, we talked at length about how and where to begin work with nursing homes. Conducting an assessment of educational needs of nurses and nursing assistants in each facility appealed to project coordinators as a useful, nonthreatening activity within which college representatives (most of whom were new to nursing homes) might come to know a nursing home staff and become known to them. Following the needs assessment (each site determined the particular form that it would take), a wide variety of staff development activities took place, depending on nursing home preferences and choices made by project staff. The variety of approaches, all of which were seen as effective, describe the many routes taken to establish and cultivate partnerships.

One or more new joint committees took shape in all six communities. Some flourished and some did not, but in every site at least one committee made up of nursing home personnel, college staff, and others from local health and education organizations emerged as an active and enduring community group. At Shoreline, an advisory committee to the project was established early and remained energetic and productive. At Triton, an Educational Planning Committee consisting of Directors of Nursing of area nursing homes and Triton faculty representatives matured into an assertive group initiating and influencing educational programs for nursing home personnel. Ohlone began with an educational planning committee which initiated staff development for nursing home aides, and continued to function as an active liaison between the college and the long-term care community. On the other hand, a project advisory committee initiated at Ohlone never came to life.

The newly formed committees reviewed results of the needs assessment and assisted in planning educational activities for college and nursing home staffs. Valencia College initiated a series of seminars and workshops on topics of mutual interest to the faculty and licensed nursing home staff, including a 445-hour gerontology course in which 20 nursing faculty and 27 nursing home RNs enrolled. The benefits of faculty and nursing home staff being together as fellow-learners went well beyond the knowledge gained in the workshop or seminar. The Community College of Philadelphia developed several short courses, meeting six or eight times each, for different levels of nursing home staff. Nursing assistants earned certificates at the end of the course; licensed nurses earned CEUs. A director of nursing support group for Philadelphia DONs emerged from a CCP planned activity, and continued to function independently. The Weber College project staff, serving a widely disbursed rural population of twelve nursing homes, developed multimedia learning modules on a variety of topics related to care of the elderly for independent use in nursing homes throughout the state of Utah. (Later marketed to a national audience.) Ohlone College offered day-long workshops on the Ohlone campus for nursing assistants—unique in that a planning committee of nursing assistants was appointed and empowered to plan the workshops. Once this small committee saw that it *really* had the responsibility of planning workshops for nursing assistants, they took up the task earnestly and enthusiastically—going so far as to interview prospective speakers before making a final selection. These workshops, held on the Ohlone campus, were popular (attracting 100 to 150 attendees each time) and much praised. At least two nursing assistants who attended later enrolled in the Ohlone nursing program, attributing their decision to the workshops which first brought them to the campus.

At other sites, workshops were held in a nursing home with invitations sent to the staffs of all nursing homes in the community. This arrangement, also novel, was appealing to participants. The host nursing home was pleased to provide hospitality and to "show off" their facility to peers. For the visiting workshop attendees, it was interesting to see another nursing home; many had never been in one other than their own. Triton College had access to microwave bands (Instructional Television Fixed Services) for delivering educational programs to local sites. The project provided receiving antenna and other hardware to participating nursing homes, and conducted a series of closed circuit educational programs on topics identified in the needs survey. Shoreline College allocated project funds to enable nursing home staff members to attend local programs at the University of Washington Geriatric Education Center. And starting a "train the trainer" approach that continued as a theme of the Shoreline project, ultimately becoming a state-wide undertaking, Shoreline staff gave workshops for nursing home staff developers on teaching, and on effective use of audiovisual materials, modeling the use of high quality video materials on subjects relating to care of the aged, which then became available for loan by the nursing homes themselves. Valencia faculty conducted small group workshops on all three shifts, on topics chosen by the staff members.

There was a kind of brokering of educational benefits that brought to nursing homes a new array of benefits, and, to some extent, brought professional nurses in participating nursing homes into the nursing mainstream. At both Ohlone and Shoreline, nurse researchers from area universities, specialists in the care of decubiti, management of Alzheimers, and other nursing problems common to the nursing home RN talked with nursing home nurses in project-sponsored conferences. In another successful brokering effort, connections between nursing home personnel and local Geriatric Education Centers were sponsored.

As project faculty spent more time in the nursing home, continuing informal and semi-formal staff education took place. As one example among many, a geropsychiatric nurse specialist on the Ohlone faculty gave a number of short on-site inservice seminars in nursing homes on topics of communication and relationships. She was unpaid, but at other sites inservice education by faculty was requested and paid for by nursing home administration. In other situations, faculty were paid with grant funds. In each of the demonstration sites efforts were made to establish collegiality, trust, and "peerness" between faculty and nursing home RNs (and LVNs in management and staff development positions). Copies of articles and meeting announcements were shared, relevant clinical information passed along, and, sometimes, conferences and meetings jointly attended. As college faculty worked with and listened to nursing home nurses, their respect and regard for them grew.

Responses to our survey of project participants at the close of the project showed that staff education activities which faculty conducted in project nursing homes were rewarding. Benefits listed by our respondents include the following:

- Faculty gained a better understanding of the nursing home, what it has and what it needs.
- Faculty became involved with staff and vice versa; this helped build an effective working relationship.

- Faculty became visible in the nursing home, at all hours, with all levels of staff, and helped the nursing home begin to feel comfortable with an academic affiliation.

- Licensed and unlicensed personnel were encouraged and supported to continue their education.

We quickly learned that one aspect of our staff development planning and budgeting was unrealistic. We had anticipated pulling nursing home staff members, including nursing assistants, away for full-day scheduled educational activities and using grant funds to reimburse the nursing home a day's wages in order that they might employ substitute workers for those attending classes. The use of substitutes is not part of the nursing home world, and employees were frequently expected to use days off for educational activities outside the facility. It is testimony to the motivation (and apparent tirelessness) of many nursing assistants that they were willing to spend days off attending project-planned continuing education courses and workshops.

Mindful of the importance of administrative support in achieving project objectives, a serious effort was made to enlist the interests of nursing home administration. In general, any interest on the part of the administrator seemed short-lived, and our sense is that while the promise of improved quality of care and recruitment through an educational affiliation attracted the initial interest of the typical nursing home administrator, the here and now demands of management in this industry soon swamp any abiding interest in educational affiliation because the benefits are relatively long-term in nature.

PEOPLE PARTNERSHIPS

One and two years after the start of the project, we became increasingly aware of the many influences that buffet the nursing home and shape day-to-day operations—federal and state regulations, changing financial structures, personnel changes in administrative and corporate offices, and, undoubtedly, other forces. It became clear that we were naive in expecting that through our best efforts we could assure a successful affiliating relationship between the nursing program and a nursing home.

We did observe, however, that long-term, stable relationships were developing with individuals, if not with organizations. There were nurses in every community who were committed to long-term care who, if they left one nursing home usually turned up working in another community facility, often calling the college to say they were at work in a new nursing home, and wished to continue an association with the project.

The idea of individual partnerships between a project staff member and a director of nursing took on shape and purpose when we decided during the first full year of the project to sponsor a workshop entitled "Blueprints for Partnership." In a report to the Foundation, we said:

> early and extensive interest in our project and its purposes has encouraged us to undertake a national meeting of persons sharing our concerns and aspirations. In a sense, this is a dissemination conference—not a dissemination of the results of a project, but dissemination of the project's perspective on the problems and dilemmas in community college-nursing home partnerships.

The topics for the workshop sessions were those we were dealing with in our partnership efforts in the six demonstration sites. For example,

- Clinical learning environments: reality vs. creativity
- Changing student interests and attitudes: preaching vs. teaching
- Staff development: sticks vs. carrots
- Faculty and professional staff development: security vs. change

All workshop sessions were presented by pairs—a nursing home RN (usually DON) and a college representative. The workshop, held in Chicago in early December 1987, was attended by 200 people, and received unusually high evaluations. Perhaps the greatest achievement of the workshop, however, was in the relationship that developed between educator and nursing home nurse as they prepared and conducted a workshop session, and what they learned about the perceptions and values each held.

We learned how little control over their own time directors of nursing in nursing homes and their assistants have. At Ohlone college, a plan called "Take a Colleague to a Conference" was announced, inviting members of the nursing program faculty to look for workshops and conferences on topics that might be of interest to a nurse working in long term care, and to invite a nurse from one of the college's partner nursing homes to attend with her. Attendance costs for both persons would be covered by grant funds. The faculty were responsive, but few nursing home nurses were able to accept the invitation, or if they did, frequently had to cancel because they were unable to leave the facility at that time. CCP faculty, and others as well, reported their dismay upon realizing how difficult it was for directors of nursing to keep scheduled meetings relating to project activities on their calendars—not for lack of interest, but for lack of control over their work time. At CCP, a DON support group grew out of a short course that CCP faculty offered for directors. The attendance at the support group, which the directors had requested, was so variable that it seemed they had to start over every time. Directors understood their isolation, and wanted relief from it.

A major undertaking, known by the acronym DACUM (Developing a Curriculum) had as an important byproduct the fostering of mutual understanding, trust, and respect between the educators and the nursing home nurses. The DACUM process, a highly structured procedure for identifying the knowledge and skills required to perform a particular work role, was undertaken to identify what needed to be taught to prepare graduates for positions in nursing homes. Following the rules of the DACUM procedure, 12 nursing home RNs (two from each demonstration site) were recruited to meet in a Chicago airport hotel for a long weekend of intense work. Under the direction of a trained leader, they listed and categorized all of the performance requirements in their work roles. Faculty did not participate, but one person from each demonstration school attended the sessions as an observer. The outcomes of the DACUM weekend ultimately defined the learning objectives for students in the nursing home clinical (Waters, 1991, pp. 74–87), and, less measurable but equally significant, strengthened the bond between the faculties of the project schools and the nurses in partner nursing homes.

Our experience in establishing partnerships was a mixture of things that worked and things that did not. Undoubtedly we missed cues or opportunities at times, and in other ways fell short in effort or skill. It became clear to us over the years of the project that the climate and culture in any one nursing home is extremely fragile and generally subject to forces more compelling than an educational affiliation. The economic and political forces driving staffing and other care-related decisions in the nursing home are powerful, usually external to the individual facility, and not in any apparent way mitigated by educational affiliations. In a Triton College summary of the demonstration phase of the project, the years 1987–1990, the project coordinator wrote:

There was a large turnover of staff in the nursing homes which meant that once we began we had to begin again and again and this was very time consuming. None of the DONs or ADONs [directors or assistant directors of nursing] that started at the beginning of the Project were in their same positions three years later. (Simmons, 1990)

Still, in each community, although the project staff had variable success maintaining specified nursing homes as learning sites, all described a great deal of success in influencing the development, growth, and enhanced professionalism of a coterie of dedicated RNs who maintain long-term care nursing careers in the community.

THE NURSING HOME
CLINICAL PLACEMENT

Project principals moved promptly to arrange student clinical placement in nursing homes, but it was months before a certain amount of uncertainty and confusion was gradually replaced by a clearer sense of place and purpose. Many preconceived ideas about affiliation with the nursing home fell away one by one. The instructional methods used to good ends in acute care settings proved unworkable in the nursing home. The criteria for selection of a student learning experience had to be re-examined, and largely discarded. An unfamiliar three-way relationship between student, nursing assistant, and the instructor became seen as the key to any student-resident relationship. Anticipated student resistance to being placed in nursing homes did not materialize. At the summing up, the misconceptions were remembered because of the good that came out of discarding them. According to the teachers, penetrating and correcting the misconceptions about the nursing home led to new, more effective ways of teaching and learning. To put it another way, project faculty came to believe that no part of the project was as powerful in transforming teaching practices as the faculty experience of creating in nursing homes a new setting for learning. One faculty member noted on her survey, "After teaching in the nursing home, faculty look at all teaching-learning methods more critically."

As they looked back on their experience, project faculty made observations about their own experiences that they believe are of help in persuading other faculty to develop affiliations in nursing homes for clinical education.

- I thought it would be easy, and was surprised that it [setting up the clinical placement] took so long, that it was so complex and hard. I kept expecting the nursing home to know what we needed to do to develop a clinical placement, and they didn't.

- They were unable to give feedback; they couldn't say how they thought we were doing, because they didn't know. They were trying so hard to please us.

- It was a surprise that some would give so much time to project activities.

- We went in expecting DONs to be like others in nursing service, but they had different needs.

- We went in on an education mode, and they were on a survival mode.

- It is culture shock for the faculty. We say an educational in-service takes an hour; they say, 'You've got 15 minutes.'

- We didn't realize how hard they work. Most are in LTC by choice; they love it and are committed to it.

- We made a mistake in going in with assumptions and color slides. The missionary model was at work here; we rushed out to save them. But we ended up getting more than we ever gave away.

Faculty began going into the nursing home at the start of the project. The project purposes argued for placing students in the nursing home for a clinical experience late in the program of study in order to prepare graduates who could take on the registered nurse role in long term care. At the start of the project, only Shoreline Community College included clinical placements in nursing homes, and that occurred during the first nursing course and had as its purpose the practice of fundamental nursing skills. In time all six demonstration programs developed last-semester clinical placement in a nursing home, but the necessary curriculum changes took longer at some sites than others. The circumstances of the curriculum additions or changes were different in each site. Community College of Philadelphia allocated a portion of the clinical time associated with a senior medical-surgical nursing course to the nursing home. As part of a large scale curriculum revision, Ohlone College created a new last-semester course to be taught in the nursing home. The Shoreline College program continued a long-standing clinical placement in nursing homes of first semester students, and redesigned a senior year management practicum to include clinical placement in nursing homes. Triton College and Weber State University began vigorous programs of continuing education and staff development in nursing homes, and only later gained faculty support in allocating clinical time to the nursing home. Valencia college promptly announced an elective clinical placement in the nursing home—available only to students who qualified for honors! During the

1986–87 school year and every year after, there were faculty members (including the coordinators/facilitators) from all six schools spending time in selected nursing homes, conducting staff education, making plans for student placement, and teaching groups of students. They talked often with each other about their experiences. Discerning, self-reflective teachers began to see the bias—verging on arrogance—present in our initial thinking about developing and using the nursing home as a clinical learning environment:

> Community College of Philadelphia faculty entered the nursing home setting ambivalent and idealistic. They were ambivalent about the value of the nursing home as a teaching site, but eager to share the expertise they felt in the planning of care and establishing standards of care. They were idealistic in that they felt they would be able to make a difference in this setting. However, faculty quickly realized that knowledge about frail older adults and a solid foundation in gerontological nursing theory was not sufficient to prepare them for the transition to teaching in the new setting. Gradually faculty discovered that they needed also to understand the environment and culture of the nursing home, both being very different from the acute care setting. The old models for practice and teaching did not transfer intact to the new setting. (Waters, 1991, pp. 29, 30)

In the 1988–89 annual report submitted to the Foundation, the Community College of Philadelphia staff wrote:

> What faculty were not prepared for was the personal role isolation that occurs in the nursing home setting. Whereas acute care settings offer faculty many role models for student learning, long-term care settings do not. Whereas acute care settings offer a rapid turnover of patients, long term care settings do not. And whereas learning in acute care settings is driven by technology and skills, learning in long term care settings is not. For faculty, role isolation in nursing home settings occurred when the familiar model of staff support, rapid client responses to change and dependence on a medical model for care were replaced by minimal professional staff support, incrementally measurable patient changes and infrequent medical support. (Community College of Philadelphia, 1989)

The CCP report describes four stages that, in their experience, faculty went through in understanding and accepting the nursing home, and reconceptualizing the teaching role in that setting (Waters, 1991) and identifies the sources of inner conflict that confront faculty. Quoting Mary Ellen Simmons at Triton College, the CCP annual report summarizes as follows:

> In identifying the faculty transitions for taking on a new role in a new setting, with all the historical and present realities that are found in that setting, faculty in their discussions have identified eight sources of conflict:
>
> 1. *Turf.* What is a faculty member's role in this setting?
> 2. *Purpose.* What can be realistically accomplished?
> 3. *Teaching Methods.* How can students be taught effectively?
> 4. *Resources.* What is available?
> 5. *Work Relationships.* Who are they with?
> 6. *Status and Power.* How can faculty be recognized and rewarded?
> 7. *Work Mastery.* How can faculty feel good about what they do?
> 8. *Group and Individual Accountability.* How can realistic goals be set and success be measured? (*Community College of Philadelphia,* 1989, p. 4)

In 1991, after a year of working actively with other colleges to help them initiate changes in clinical and classroom teaching about gerontology, a staff meeting was dedicated to sharing the outcomes of Year One of dissemination. The minutes of that meeting list the common experiences members of the project staff were having as they met with other faculties. A common question: What about the lack of role models in the nursing home? With a smile, and exaggerating for effect, one person reported the commonly expressed concerns about the nursing home—"it lacks equipment, dollars, doctors, nurses, skills, linen, soap, and gloves." The grins and amused discussion which followed revealed that once project staff members themselves had been worried about just such things, but that now, after four years of placing students in nursing homes, such concerns were seen as trivial and not substantively important to the learning experience. We had come to see how our first approaches to the nursing home were biased and how, had the bias not been corrected, our attitudes would have been a prelude to failure. A major breakthrough for faculty came with perceiving the bias and developing new and changed attitudes and practices toward the nursing home and the nurses and nursing assistants who work there. It became clear to faculty they had defined what they expected in a clinical placement in terms of the acute care hospital. In Chapter 5, Hanson discusses the changes that occurred in our evaluation protocol as we came to grips with our erroneous and uninformed thinking about nursing homes.

WHAT MAKES A PARTNERSHIP SUCCESSFUL?

From the beginning, the W. K. Kellogg Foundation had a particular interest in our efforts to form partnerships with the nursing homes. In correspondence relating to the plans for the survey to learn the perceptions of persons affiliated with the project about its successes and shortcomings, Helen Grace, speaking for the Foundation, said, "I would have interest in . . . insights into factors that facilitated or hindered development of the partnership efforts in and of themselves. . . . We have an interest in learning more about what contributes to successful partnership development."

We have tried to look critically at the factors that accounted for successes and failures in our collaboration with nursing homes, and to compare our experiences and findings with characteristics of successful partnerships described in current writing on the topic. An examination of the factors that characterized the community college-nursing home partnerships in relation to other findings is useful; nursing education in the future may be expected to seek new "partners" in education, and the nursing home experience may offer directions more or less likely to foster success.

What makes a partnership work? As noted in the opening paragraph of this chapter, this question emerged early in our project, and prompted a study by an advisory committee member, a CCP faculty member, and two members of the project staff. The study found the following list of factors to be associated with a successful partnership between a community college ADN program and a nursing home:

1. Expectations for students' clinical experiences should be clear, written, and discussed with the nursing home staff.
2. Clinical learning experiences in the nursing home for nursing students should provide opportunities for the student to develop respect for the elderly and an understanding of the nursing home setting.

3. The community college and the nursing home should believe that education can make a difference.

4. A thorough orientation of the community college faculty and students to the nursing home should occur.

5. The partnership should be committed to and involved in providing high quality services to the elderly.

6. Partnership goals should be realistic, achievable, and practical.

7. Faculty and nursing home staff should be knowledgable about gerontology and value the worth of clinical practice in gerontology.

8. The partnership should develop a plan to keep communication channels open, adequate, and current.

9. The partnership should be committed to high quality education.

10. Administrators at both sites should have demonstrated commitment to and interest in development of students and staff.

11. The community college and the nursing home should demonstrate understanding and respect for each other's mission, goals, responsibilities and environments whether or not they relate to partnership activities.

12. The community college and the nursing home should demonstrate commitment to ongoing education of personnel.

13. Student learning experiences should include a clear understanding of the role of the registered nurse in the nursing home.

14. Faculty should be knowledgable about gerontology and the patients their students care for in the nursing home.

15. The community college and the nursing home should share responsibilities for making the partnership work.

16. Time should be provided to plan, implement and evaluate partnership activities. (Mengel, Simson, Sherman, & Waters, 1991)

Duplicating or overlapping many of the Mengel factors, a review of research literature about collaboration finds these more generally stated factors repeatedly cited as being necessary for a successful partnership:

1. There is a history of collaboration or cooperation in the community.

2. Mutual respect, understanding, and trust is demonstrated.

3. Partner organizations provide an appropriate cross section of members to implement the new venture.

4. Members see collaboration as in their self-interest.

5. Members share a stake in both process and outcome.

6. Multiple layers of collaborative groups participate in decision making.

7. Flexibility is demonstrated.

8. Open and frequent communication occurs.

9. Both informal and formal communication lines are established.

10. The established goals and objectives are concrete and attainable.

11. There is a shared vision.

12. There are sufficient funds.

13. A skilled convener is found (Mattessich & Monsey, 1992).

Drawing on still another source, the subject of collaboration between nursing homes and educational organizations came up briefly at an NLN-sponsored conference attended by this author. In the discussion, the Executive Director of the American Health Care Association offered a short, clear-cut set of criteria for a "total partnership":

1. Both partners sit in on policy and strategic planning at corporate levels.

2. Faculty are present and participate in human resource development and allocation.

3. The delivery system organization contracts for faculty time.

4. There is a long-term (5 year) plan.

5. At all levels of each organization resources in the other organization are available and can be obtained by a phone call (Wildging, 1992).

This shorter list of criteria, which we might call the Wildging list, sharpens an analysis of the project partnerships. None of these criteria were fully met in the partnerships developed under the project. There were activities, however, which were intended to move us in the direction of these criteria, and an account of our efforts in relation to the Wildging criteria may be useful to educators and nursing home nurses who undertake the development of new affiliations.

1. Both Partners Sit in on Policy and Strategic Planning at Corporate Levels

The most that can be said for our efforts is that we did seek and pursue avenues of communication with the nursing home industry at corporate levels and at national and state levels. We were in a better position to develop lines of communication than we might otherwise have been because of two sets of choices. First, following Helen Grace's early advice, we solicited the participation of nursing home industry representatives on the advisory board, and second, as a member of the NLN Board during the demonstration project years, the author pursued contacts made possible by carrying an active role on the Board's Long-Term Care Committee. In addition, project coordinators at each of the sites initiated contact with state nursing home trade associations, governmental regulatory agencies, and state organizations of physicians and others who provide services in nursing homes. (There were extended and salutory consequences at some sites, described in Chapter 5.)

The communication lines allowed a much wider distribution of informational and educative project materials. The 12,000 nursing homes on the mailing list of the American Health Care Association received materials describing the benefits and methods of establishing an educational affiliation with a school of nursing and letters from the executive staff urging action on the part of the nursing home. Project directors and coordinators received and responded to invitations to participate in national and regional nursing home industry conferences and workshops, and to write for nursing home trade journals. We would be hard pressed to provide any documentation, but we are convinced that the rapid increase in the number of community college-nursing home partnerships (for clinical affiliation purposes) between 1990 and 1993 (Hanson, 1992, 1994; also, appendix B) occurred in part because at the same time that we were working closely with our colleagues in ADN education to further goals of the project, we aggressively pursued any platform that was offered us by the nursing home industry.

2. Faculty Are Present and Participate in Human Resource Development and Allocation

Project staff participated actively in human resource development, including efforts such as the Shoreline "train the trainer" series of workshops given across the state of Washington for staff developers in nursing homes.

3. The Delivery System Organization
Contracts for Faculty Time

In the beginning, we envisioned college-nursing home partnerships which would lead to joint appointments—a faculty position partly supported by the nursing home and partly by the college in which an educator would teach in both settings as well as perform liaison services for student placement. A joint appointment was realized at one site only—Valencia College, it was of short duration—one year, and grant funds provided the nursing home portion of the salary.

Nursing homes did, however, contract for faculty time to conduct staff development classes. A large portion of the staff development carried out by faculty was done without charge to the nursing home, but other classes were requested and paid for by the nursing home.

4. There Is a Long-Term (5-Year) Plan

In one sense, the written agreement for student placement represents a plan; such agreements are commonly reviewed and approved by executive officers at the college and in the nursing home. But in the sense that Wildging probably intended, no long term plans were developed.

5. At All Levels of Each Organization
Resources in the Other Organization Are
Available and Can Be Obtained by a Phone Call

There were reciprocal events in the sharing of educational resources which fit this criterion, although the requests and responses typically occurred between the offices of the director of nursing at the nursing home and the program director or project faculty of the college.

There were no "total partnerships" in the Wildging sense, and a limited number that met all of the criteria listed by Mengel and by Mattessich and Monsey. New collaborative arrangements to meet educational needs were achieved at every project site, however, and partners with no history of association found mutually beneficial ways of working together.

Collaboration is a mutually beneficial and well-defined relationship entered into by two or more organizations to achieve common goals. The relationship includes a commitment to: a definition of mutual relationships and goals; a jointly developed structure and shared responsibility; mutual authority and accountability for success; and sharing of resources and rewards. (Mattessich & Monsey, 1992)

Reviewing the activities which made up our efforts to establish collaborative relationships with nursing homes, and measuring our achievements against criteria that have been developed for partnerships lead us to offer a list of suggestions which others might follow in developing new affiliations with nursing homes. A number of these suggestions come from project staff responses to our survey form question, "In terms of your college's partnership with a nursing home, discuss the factors that facilitated and hindered the development and maintenance of a partner relationship" . . . Also, in your opinion, "what are the essential characteristics of a successful partnership between two structurally unrelated organizations, such as a community college and a nursing home?" (Survey form is found in Appendix D.) Ann Carignan, project coordinator at Valencia College, responded with a full list of "essential characteristics of a successful partnership," and many of the items on this list of suggestions are hers.

LESSONS LEARNED ABOUT DEVELOPING A SUCCESSFUL PARTNERSHIP WITH A NURSING HOME

1. Meet with nursing home administrator and the director of nursing and ask for an explicit discussion of what benefits each party sees in the partnership. Identify mutual goals.
2. Identify resources each has to contribute to the partnership and plan how they will be shared and used. Plan to share facilities, resources, and people as much as you can to strengthen ties.
3. Be clear about what you will do and what you would like them to do. Make no assumptions.
4. Go in with and ask for willingness to explore, to try something as a pilot.
5. Designate a primary contact person/liaison from the college, and ask that one be designated at the nursing home.
6. Plan to mentor the nursing home staff (they may feel uninformed about nursing education and be afraid to say so) and ask the nursing home staff to mentor the faculty (most of them are uninformed

about nursing homes and long term care, and uneasy about asking nursing home nurses to enlighten them).

7. Expect frustrations; keep your overall goal clear in your mind.

8. Avoid taking defeats and frustrations personally by looking at the process, at the goals, at the strategies. Stay away from "them vs. us" thinking.

9. Be honest.

10. Meet regularly, but keep the meetings brief. Push for faculty involvement in nursing home meetings and committees.

11. Develop a brief handbook for the nursing home staff new to a student affiliation. Include a brief overview of the nursing curriculum. Describe the student and faculty roles in plain language, and suggest the role that nursing home staff might play. Give down-to-earth hints about how nursing assistants can contribute to the student's learning experience.

12. Go over the clinical evaluation tool with nursing home staff. Make a summary in every day English of the primary criteria of acceptable clinical performance—what it is that is most important to your faculty.

13. Wherever possible, help faculty (or yourself) take up roles on committees and advisory boards in the nursing home.

14. Explore the possibility of faculty teaching courses for nursing home staff through the college's continuing education program. Where this is feasible, faculty learn more about the skills and educational needs of staff, and staff become more aware of faculty talents, with the result that respect is heightened on both sides.

15. Remind yourself that the nursing home staff wants desperately to be understood.

REFERENCES

Community College of Philadelphia. (1989, March). Annual report to the W.K. Kellogg Foundation. Philadelphia: The Community College of Philadelphia, p. 2.

Hanson, H. A. (1992, Winter). Highlights of the national survey: Gerontological nursing in the ADN curriculum. Newslink.

Hanson, H. A. (1994, Winter). Changes in gerontological curriculum content and clinical learning experiences 1990–1993. *Newslink*.

Mattessich, P. W., & Monsey, B. R. (1992). *Collaboration: What makes it work. A review of research literature on factors influencing successful collaboration*. St. Paul: Amherst H. Wilder Foundation.

Mengel, A., Simson, S., Sherman, S., & Waters, V. (1991). Essential factors in a community college-nursing home partnership. *Journal of Gerontological Nursing, 16*:11, 26–31.

Simmons, M. E. (1990, August). Triton College executive summary: The Community College Nursing Home Partnership, 9-1-87 to 8-31-1990. Oak Grove, IL: Triton College.

Waters, V. (Ed.). (1991). *Teaching gerontology*. New York: National League for Nursing Press.

Wildging, P. (1992). Conference notes taken by author at the National League for Nursing International Conference on Long-Term Care. Montauk, New York.

4

Influencing the Nursing Community and Beyond: New Resources, New Constituencies

From the beginning we intended to reach outside our own settings to interact with organizations and agencies which influence nursing homes and the nurses who work in them, but we expected to concentrate on demonstrating the "how to" during the first three year period, and, assuming that it went well, to request funding for a second project to disseminate "lessons learned" (the phrase used in Kellogg Foundation literature). In line with that long-range plan, the demonstration phase proposal included the following objective, "To develop plans for dissemination of findings to associate degree nursing educators, nursing homes, and other nurses working in the long-term care field." A two-day work session devoted to developing ideas for the dissemination project was held in May 1989. Not only were the program directors at all six demonstration sites interested in continuing with a dissemination project, but the faculty carrying project roles were also eager to share their work of the preceding 2.5 years with their colleagues in other schools. We scheduled a special session to work on development of a dissemination project partly because we felt the best ideas about dissemination would derive from the direct experience of the staff members responsible for demonstration activities in each school, but for another reason as well: It provided an opportunity for members of the staff to learn, or learn more about designing and developing a project proposal for grant funding.

Seventeen project principals—directors of the six nursing programs, the project coordinators and other faculty assigned to work with the project, and Helen Hanson (project evaluator), Susan Sherman, and I—participated. A set of questions to be discussed was mailed out in advance.

1. What outcomes of your project do you feel the most proud of?
2. Can other colleges do the same thing? If so, why should they?
3. What project activities at your site will be in existence after grant funding is over?
4. What has been most difficult for you to accomplish? Which new ideas met the most resistance? What took more time than you expected? What have you started that never took hold? What couldn't be brought under control?
5. What of all your project activities are the best ideas for the future? Have the best chance of lasting?
6. Who else would benefit from such a future and might help to bring it about?

Most of the first day was spent responding to these questions. Large sheets of newsprint were hung on the walls and an outline of the discussion was recorded with broad-tipped pens. The recorded notes remained hanging on the walls around the room for the two days, creating a visual group memory of main points. When discussion prompted by the six questions seemed more or less complete, the large group broke up into 4 task groups of 3 or 4 persons each. Each task group was asked to design a dissemination project based on the discussion that had just occurred. Each group was asked to specify the following: purposes of the dissemination project, the intended audience, proposed activities, anticipated outcomes, timeline, and resources needed. Each task group completed its work by outlining the proposal on newsprint and making a presentation to the entire group. A lively discussion of the merits of various ideas in the four proposals followed. The final proposal (written by Sherman and Waters and approved by project staff at each site) funded by the Foundation some months later was based directly on the ideas developed in that work session. A secondary, but important and equally intentional benefit was the education in project analysis and development which the work session provided.

The dissemination proposal to the Foundation (see Appendix A) listed the following major purposes.

1. To develop dissemination resource materials, including a videotape and curriculum handbook.

2. To provide conferences, workshops, and consultation at six regional centers to share strategies and skills with associate degree nursing educators and nursing home personnel.

3. To collaborate with other organizations, including regional Geriatric Education Centers (GECs), the National League for Nursing (NLN), the American Nurses Association (ANA), the National Gerontological Nursing Association (NGNA), the American Society of Allied Health Professionals (ASAHP), the American Association of Community and Junior Colleges (AACJC), the American Health Care Association (AHCA), and the American Association of Homes for the Aging (AAHA), in conference and workshop programming which draws upon and extends demonstration site experiences.

4. To monitor and influence, insofar as possible, changing patterns in NCLEX-RN examination, state rules and regulations governing nursing curricula, evolving competency statements from NLN education councils and changing accreditation criteria in relationship to the redirection of Associate Degree Nursing curriculum.

To a large extent, these purposes were realized. In the discussion that follows, I hope to highlight some of the less common outreach activities as examples of avenues that open to nursing faculty when an active community role is expected. It should also be said that the present faculty workload in community college nursing programs makes community time hard to come by. In recounting the community contacts made during the conduct of our project, we recognize that such extensive community involvement on the part of a faculty member is possible only when funds from sources outside the average departmental budget are available.

From the time we first began talking about the project, we envisioned extensive interaction with the communities of nursing education, long-term care nursing, and major nursing organizations. Then, as noted in Chapter 1, when the project was approved for funding by the W. K. Kellogg Foundation, Dr. Helen Grace urged us to expand our thinking about the project to seek linkages "beyond the nursing component of community colleges to other areas of study and beyond nursing homes to broader based community settings." Dr. Grace's advice substantially influenced the scope of project activities; in every demonstration site project, faculty developed associations with agencies and organizations devoted to elder care outside the usual realms of either nursing education or nursing home care. It was an important redirection. Without the encouragement contained in Dr. Grace's comment, we would not only have not sought wide-ranging involvement, we might have resisted it to some extent for fear of distracting ourselves from what we first defined as the main purpose. But in the course of the project many opportunities emerged, and project coordinators and other faculty members became active in work groups outside of nursing that were dedicated to advancing the cause of elder care and well-being. They often found they were able to make a substantive contribution to the work being done; the nursing perspective was at times important to decisions and to the resolution of issues. In other instances, the project itself served as a broker, bringing groups together to find mutually agreeable solutions to problems that were straining relationships. Examples are cited later in this chapter. But first I will review project efforts to establish a presence within the nursing community for the purpose of spreading the project message; the success of these efforts is due to many factors, including the nursing community's readiness to engage with the topic of gerontology. But the energy and creativity of project staff in promotion, coalition-building, collaboration, and information-sharing in the nursing community contributed to success, and the approaches they used could be applied to other educational change purposes.

INFLUENCING THE NURSING COMMUNITY

From the beginning, throughout the demonstration phase, project principals and other faculty at the six college sites sought involvement in local organizations serving the interests of long-term care nurses, sought opportunities to speak to nursing groups about the project, and wrote about what they were doing for newsletters and magazines. Local and national units of the National League for Nursing and the American Nurses Association were approached for support along with other professional associations with an investment in basic nursing education. In those first three years, the base of involvement steadily widened. For most (perhaps all) of the project coordinators and faculty, public speaking and writing for publication represented a new challenge. They rose to the challenge, learning from and supporting each other. The public speaking skills of project staff members and other faculty increased, and teams of presenters from different colleges evolved. Individual speakers and teams became popular with the audiences of a particular organization, and were invited to speak at several regional and national sessions sponsored by that organization. Project principals whose salary was funded by the Foundation did not receive a speaker's fee (which may have added to their attractiveness as speakers), but they asked for travel expenses as needed in relation to the college's grant budget. A guiding decision made early in the project was that we would share freely among ourselves and with all others any course, curriculum, and clinical teaching materials developed within the project effort. As speakers at meetings, project principals prepared handouts, responded to requests for materials, and referred requests to other demonstration sites. Across the country, course descriptions and outlines, learning activities for the nursing home clinical experience, and other teaching materials were distributed freely among nurse educators and, in so far as possible, among nurses working in long term care. The deliberate decision to treat all curriculum materials developed within the project as seed to be sown and scattered must have influenced the rapid spread of curriculum change in associate degree curriculums. In the year following the end of funding and formal project activities, demonstration site faculty attending a national meeting reported recognizing curriculum materials they had developed now being distributed by a conference speaker. Such experiences have been a source of satisfaction.

Project principals at the six sites expanded their involvement in the larger nursing community in a wide range and variety of activities. The project coordinator at Triton College became co-convenor for a Community College Study Group within AGHE, and provided consultation to a nearby technical college with an AGHE grant. At Valencia College, four faculty members became NLN site visitors, the program director was appointed to a statewide committee on gerontological issues in education and health, and the coordinator participated actively in a local group of nursing home directors of nursing as well as in other local and state organizations. In her response survey at the end of the project the Valencia project coordinator observed, "The project changed the whole structure and operation of the college's clinical affiliations. We were provided entry with ease into the inner circle of clinical organizations. Trust increased on both sides. As those of us representing the school were more willing to reveal needs, be more honest, there was more honesty and candor on all sides. Changed the advisory committee role. More involvement."

One of the Shoreline coordinators was elected to the CADP Board of Review for NLN accreditation and the other took on a new and active role in NLN. From Weber College the coordinator was appointed to the editorial board of *Geriatric Nursing*. Principals at Community College of Philadelphia and Ohlone College, similarly, took on active organizational roles. The CCP coordinator became a widely sought speaker on the teaching role in nursing homes, and the Ohlone coordinator became active in influential policy organizations shaping gerontology education and nursing home operations in the state. The project gained visibility, stature, and thus effectiveness by the range and quality of project faculty participation in community activities.

We believe that an assertive effort to ally the project with the National League for Nursing's programming in long-term care also enhanced success. During the life of the project, the two project administrators, Susan Sherman and I, carried active roles in the National League for Nursing, including (between us) membership on the Board of Governors, Council chairmanship, and member and chair positions on Long-Term Care and Accreditation Committees. We were able to interlace project purposes and organizational goals, serving NLN as well as the project. As a member of an NLN committee to revise criteria for the accreditation of associate degree programs, Susan Sherman gathered support for explicit reference to the importance of education for nurses which prepares for elder care. During the dissemination phase, three highly rated workshops were jointly sponsored and supported by the National League for Nursing and the project. We sought publication of the teacher handbooks, *Teaching Gerontology* and its companion *Resource Guide*, and this final project publication as well, by NLN press. We also elected to approach the NLN Communications Division to become our partners in the production of the video, *Time to Care*. With a marketing and distribution system in place, NLN was in a better position to promote widespread use of the video than any of the project colleges were (or would want to become). The assumption that we were strengthening our ability to influence the nursing community by an alliance with NLN was verified in a number of ways, including a written comment from a nurse educator that the visible affiliation between the project and the NLN lent credibility and persuasiveness to the project agenda.

PRODUCING A VIDEOTAPE
AND A HANDBOOK

Work began in the summer of 1990 on what would become an award-winning videotape, *Time to Care*, and a teacher's handbook, *Teaching Gerontology*, that was selected as an AJN book of the year. Belying the common wisdom about the loss of efficiency when a committee makes a product, both the videotape and the handbook are the work of a committee of eight—one person from each of the demonstration sites, Sherman, and this author. The group spent two days in suburban

Philadelphia in September, 1990 laying out the general plans for the book and the videotape. Questions were again used to stimulate discussion among the site representatives, each of whom had been coordinating demonstration projects for three years. Questions posed included:

- Why should the nursing curriculum change to increase the teaching of gerontology?
- Why is the nursing home the best place to teach certain concepts?
- How does teaching in the nursing home differ from teaching in the acute hospital?
- What are the challenges in teaching in the nursing home?

A list of major topics to be included in the book was generated, with each person indicating those they felt best qualified to write about. By the end of the work session, ideas coalesced into usable plans for each publication. This author, executive director of the videotape and editor of the handbook, provided feedback to the committee as the video script took shape and production began, and worked closely with the six authors of the handbook chapters.

The National League for Nursing published both the videotape and the handbook, and a later collection of teaching resources.

A BROADER FRONT FOR THE
COMMUNITY COLLEGE

Each demonstration site found college departments and services other than nursing interested in expanding contacts with the community in the field of gerontology. Project coordinators at each campus announced the grant award in one way or another to their campus community, describing the plans for a nursing program-nursing home partnership, and inviting other departments to explore with project staff any ideas they might have for activities to promote the well-being of older citizens in the community.

At Ohlone College, the Early Childhood Education program faculty expressed immediate interest in an intergenerational project. Working together, the ECS department chair and the project coordinator inaugurated the "Grand Pal" program, teaming the 4- and 5-year-olds in the ECS preschool and a self-selected group of residents at the nearby Masonic Home.

Meeting alternately at the campus pre-school and the retirement facility, the children and the seniors engaged in craft projects, themed holiday events, and story-telling and listening. The Grand Pal program, now in its eighth year of operation, is a valued, apparently stable part of the Early Childhood curriculum at Ohlone, and the chairperson of the ECS program has become something of an expert among early childhood educators on setting up an intergenerational program.

Our experiences showed that there are a number of ways in which the nursing faculty, often without great expenditures of time, can help other programs in the community college modify programs and services to make them more reflective of and responsive to the aging population. Most community colleges offer a variety of career training programs in the health field. Not surprisingly, most of those curriculums, like nursing, have been slow to provide instruction related to the special needs of clients who are older and frail. As part of efforts to widen the scope of project activities, project staff and faculty in the six demonstration programs worked with other health career programs to improve gerontologic nursing instruction, and provide clinical learning assignments in long-term care settings. The nursing program director at Shoreline College initiated classroom and clinical instruction for dental hygiene students; similarly Community College of Philadelphia, Valencia, and Ohlone College provided specialized instruction in care of older clients to students of dental hygiene, dental assisting, respiratory therapy, and medical office assisting.

One further example of possibilities that might be explored by readers: at Ohlone College, two members of the English faculty became interested in exploring the literature which contributes to an understanding of aging and the aged. They developed a proposal for a small state grant (which they did not receive) that would have provided time to conduct a literature survey and make recommendations to the English department for more "age sensitive" reading and writing assignments.

NEW COMMUNITY PATHWAYS FOR NURSE EDUCATORS

The point of view that individual projects would be open to whatever community roles might be called for led to new levels of involvement in community organizations promoting elder care. Triton College responded to a request from the State Department of Public Health to jointly provide continuing education workshops for Nursing Home Administrators.

Because of state funding problems, the Public Health Department was unable to continue joint sponsorship after 1992. The college elected to continue offering the workshops with the state representatives continuing in an advisory capacity for program planning. On a topic identified by the state as important, namely, infection control in nursing homes, tension existed between nursing home administrators and regulatory body surveyors. The college turned to a CDC publication for clarification, and then gave workshops for nursing home administrators and regulatory board surveyers in joint attendance. Seven hundred administrators and 130 regulatory agency employees attended and, based on discussions at the workshop (with OBRA, the state health department, and other concerned parties represented) state regulations were changed to the mutual satisfaction of the interested parties.

At an early meeting of the advisory board, member Richard Besdine urged project sites to assertively seek an affiliation with the nearest Geriatric Education Center. Out of his direct involvement at the federal level he described a little realized charge that GEC projects extend their activities to community colleges. We followed his advice, with uneven and interesting results. Responses to our overtures ranged from none to enthusiastic. The Ohlone project coordinator became active partners with two GECs, one at the University of Southern California and the other at Stanford University. In joint sponsorship with USC, a series of very well-attended workshops was offered to California nursing faculty to update their knowledge and skill for teaching gerontological nursing.

The Stanford University Geriatric Education Project addressed the needs of aging members of minority populations (ethnogeriatrics), and an extensive and fruitful relationship developed between the staffs of the Ohlone project and the Stanford GEC. A number of jointly sponsored training programs for nursing home employees, nurse educators, and other constituencies were jointly sponsored by the two projects. The Ohlone project coordinator had, in the assessment of nursing home staff training needs, identified as an area of concern problems in communication and decision making among members of culturally diverse nursing home staffs. Knowing that the focus of the Stanford GEC was on ethnogeriatric issues, the Ohlone coordinator asked Stanford whether they could provide any solutions for the nursing home staff interethnic conflicts. Stanford project faculty collected data through questionnaires and interviews, then developed educational programs to improve communication and decision-making skills of the multiethnic staff.

There are more examples than will be mentioned here of the wide-ranging involvement of project principals in elder care issues that went beyond the usual borders nurse educators designate for themselves. In moving beyond the nursing component to participate in community discussions about care for the elderly, faculty found new, broadened meaning in their role as educators. They widened their horizons, developed new skills and interests, and established new patterns of professional activity which continue beyond the project. Without the added funding for dissemination, the impact of the project would not have been as great. On the other hand, without the vigorous effort to demonstrate approaches to curriculum change, and the careful attention to the processes and side effects of change activities, we would have had less to disseminate. And last, without the prodding by Helen Grace, the Foundation representative, we would have defined ourselves narrowly, and made less of a difference.

5

The Role of Evaluation:
The "How" as Well as the "How Much"

INTRODUCTION

The Kellogg Foundation makes it clear in proposal guidelines, in correspondence up to and including the approval letter and in subsequent contacts that evaluation is a necessary part of a funded project. While a clear and effective evaluation design is important, the Foundation acknowledges that a design can be so rigid as to place severe constraints on a program and some systematic evaluation practices will capture little of the rich experiences of a successful project. (Council on Foundations, 1993a, p. 232.) The Foundation made it clear to us that evaluation should be used to see problems more clearly, and to share the "lessons learned" in moving through the problems.

The participation from the beginning of the project evaluator in project discussions and major decisions was an important source of strength. A number of the evaluation activities were carried out by project faculty under the direction of the evaluator, reflecting the philosophy expressed by the evaluator of another educational change project:

For an institution such as a public school district to change and progress, the teachers, principals, superintendent, and other school personnel need to feel some personal ownership of whatever processes of change the undertake, be clear about what they are trying to accomplish, and have their own dependable measures of success and failure. How? Make everyone an evaluator and give them an evaluation design that is emminently practical, convenient, and stimulating. (Council on Foundations, 1993b, p. 92)

Helen Hanson, the project evaluator, developed and carried out an evaluation design that was practical, convenient, and stimulating—and instructive to all members of the project group in how to think about the relationship between goals, activities, and outcomes. As a companion to the evaluation plan, she introduced the staff to a way of planning that she called the Implementation Plan.

Objective Addressed	What It Would Be Like if the Activity Was Successful (Intended Outcome)	Participants	Activities to Accomplish Intended Outcome	Who Is Responsible	When It Will Occur

As she describes in the main text of this chapter, which follows this brief introduction, the process of working with an implementation plan promotes "clarity of plans based on reality." She helped faculty to be concrete in identifying how they would meet general goals. As she describes below, she functioned as a facilitator, an interpreter, and a motivator. Seen as a consultant and advisor instead of as an auditor, her participation and feedback was held to be important, and project staff observed in retrospect that she functioned more as an educator than as an evaluator. In reporting its view of the evaluation component of funded projects, the Kellogg Foundation observes that a grant is expected to leave an organization stronger in its ability to use evaluation (Council on Foundations, 1993a, p. 240) and that it should emphasize evaluation methods that "affirm and reflect rather than compare and contrast"

(Council on Foundations, 1993a, p. 250). We believe Helen Hanson's participation in the project as evaluator enabled us to meet those standards. Her report which follows explains how.

EVALUATION AS PLANNING
Helen A. Hanson, PhD, RN

In many special projects, evaluation focuses primarily, if not only, on determining to what extent the project meets its objectives. The external evaluator typically assists those writing the grant proposal to operationally define objectives and outcome variables for measurement and selects or develops the instruments to measure them. The evaluator then carries out the baseline data collection and disappears until the end of the project when data are obtained again, hopefully showing intended changes. With this approach, the funding agency learns whether or not its money accomplished its purpose and the project staff and recipients obtain a measure of their efforts.

What an outcome evaluation does not provide, however, is information about factors that contribute to or interfere with achievement of project goals. Consequently, others interested in replicating a particular project design or effort learn little about such matters as the administrative matrix that guided the project or problems encountered and how project staff dealt with them. This monograph is intended to provide that information by telling the story of the Partnership Project. In this chapter, I, the evaluation consultant throughout the seven years of project support, describe my role as evaluator and how evaluation not only served to measure and report outcomes, but contributed to the explication and evolution of the project. It is hoped that the following profile of the partnership between planning and evaluation that characterized the project will lead others to better utilize and evaluators in their special projects.

In the Partnership Project, the role of the evaluator and evaluation was as evident in initial planning and ongoing shaping and development of the project as it was in the final outcome evaluation studies, which are reported in Appendix B and elsewhere (Hanson, 1994a, 1994b; Hanson & Waters, 1991). A number of factors influenced the multifaceted role of evaluation in the project.

The initial phase (1986–1990) was funded as a demonstration project. Therefore, in addition to determining to what extent the goals were achieved (outcome evaluation), the demonstration project carried with it the obligation to identify implications for replication. This need to learn what one could about what works, or does not work, under what conditions requires an ongoing analysis of project operations, often referred to as process evaluation. Moreover, it is this evaluation of the process of the project, in light of the project outcomes, that is usually the key to implications for replication. In order to maximize the evaluator's contribution to process evaluation and to conclusions regarding implications for replication, this project was planned and budgeted for the evaluator to be an active participant in project staff discussions and activities throughout the project period.

The design of the proposed project also influenced evaluation plans and the role of the evaluator. The grant proposal was written as a national "umbrella project" with six diverse and geographically-dispersed ADN programs submitting proposals with the same general goals and objectives. The individual projects were expected to identify how each program was going to meet those objectives in the unique settings and circumstances of their colleges and communities. Although the individual grant proposals suggested possible activities aimed at the objectives, funding was initiated before definitive "activity plans" were required. This decision by the W. K. Kellogg Foundation, probably based on the track record of the national project administrator and the soundness of the overall project design, had a significant impact on the shaping and success of the partnership projects. Most importantly, it allowed for an initial staff meeting in the Spring of 1987 at which project staff from the six projects discussed activities each expected to carry out to meet the objectives. During these discussions, they identified their strengths that would facilitate accomplishment and potential problems that may occur. This openness to sharing and discussing as yet unformulated plans set the stage for an atmosphere of sharing and mutuality that grew and became a notable strength of the project. Also, as intended, that initial meeting gave the evaluation consultant a timely opportunity to present a framework for each site to map project implementation and evaluation plans and to participate in discussions of how each project site might approach each objective.

Characteristics of the person chosen as the project evaluator strongly influenced the role evaluation played in the project. As a nursing educator with an emphasis in evaluation and experience in project evaluation, I had worked with the project administrator as the evaluation consultant to a number of other projects she administered. Because of her familiarity with my philosophy of evaluation, abilities and style, she knew that evaluation in this project would be more than an audit of outcomes. This knowledge of what an evaluator can offer a project, and the project administrator's respect for evaluation and the evaluator's abilities play a key role in effective project evaluation. In the Partnership Project, my participation was taken seriously by the staff from the very beginning, due at least in part to the respect accorded me by the highly regarded project administrator.

THE EVALUATOR AS PLANNER

When the enthusiastic group of project staff members met for the first time in 1987, they were delighted with the honor of receiving the grants and full of ideas for activities to launch their partnership projects. Even though evaluation understandably was not high on their priority list at the time, a two-hour workshop on evaluation as a tool for project planning took place following the discussion about possible activities to meet each of the project's objectives. The importance of the timing of this workshop experience cannot be understated in view of the characteristics of the staff and the flexibility allowed by the grant in pursuing the goals.

Granted, all of the administrative staff of the six partnerships were experienced nursing educators, and almost all previously worked with, if not administered special project grants. However, the challenge of this particular project was unlike any other. Just how could a small group of individuals establish working partnerships between two types of organizations as different as nursing homes and community colleges, and change the attitudes of faculty and students toward a matter as undesirable as aging and the nursing home? In spite of the magnitude of the challenge, and the lack of forerunners to learn from, project staff from each site brought to the planning meeting dozens of creative ideas for activities aimed at changing attitudes and relationships. However, without some basis for organizing and focusing their ideas for activities, these creative, highly motivated individuals could become overwhelmed by what they would take on.

Therefore, I conducted a brief evaluation workshop focusing on project development strategies that promoted clarity of plans based on reality. In making the case for using evaluation for decision making and priority setting, a framework for an individualized Implementation Plan guided by the common goals and objectives was presented as a common tool for each project to outline how it would address each objective. For each objective, the individual projects would identify in a horizontal format: (1) Intended Outcomes; (2) Targeted Participants; (3) Activities to

Accomplish Intended Outcomes; (4) Persons Responsible; and (5) When Activities Would Occur. For example, one objective of this project could be operationally defined and mapped through the steps of the Implementation Plan grid as follows:

Objective:	Develop cooperative activities (between ADN program and nursing homes) aimed at improving the quality of patient care.
Intended Outcomes:	A minimum of two education programs each year to be offered to NH staff.
Targeted Participants:	Nursing home staff: RNs, LPNs, Aides
Activities:	Administer educational needs survey to staff
	Survey NH directors of nursing and project advisory committee
	Analyze data and prioritize staff educational needs
	Plan, develop and schedule classes to each shift of staff
Persons Responsible:	Project Director and Lead Faculty
When to Occur:	Survey October 1987
	Classes January 1988–April 1990

At first, the project staff appeared to be as overwhelmed at this initial meeting by the task of producing a detailed implementation plan as they were of the overall challenge of the project to "redirect ADN education." However, although it may appear to outsiders to be mere busy-work, staff later looked on development of the plan as a valuable experience that helped them to be concrete in identifying exactly how and when they were to meet project goals. As intended, the process of decision making that went into developing the plan was more valuable than the plan itself. Staff later said that it promoted a way of thinking about project activities and served as a guide for priority setting among the many ideas generated for activities, all of which could not be accomplished in available time and resources.

The Implementation Plan also served as the essential basis for its companion Evaluation Plan developed by each project. Based upon the "intended outcomes" identified in the Implementation Plan, the framework for the Evaluation Plan included, for each outcome: (1) Measures of Success; (2) Source of Data; (3) Instrumentation; (4) Date of Collection; and (5) Person Responsible. The evaluation guide for the sample project objective mapped out above for implementation would look something like the following:

Outcome Variable:	Inservice classes for NH staff
Measure of Success:	Minimum of two classes per year offered each shift to at least 80 percent of NH staff
Source of Data:	Faculty teaching inservice class and NH director of nursing
Instrumentation:	Class attendance records and NH staffing records
Date of Collection:	Annually in May
Person Responsible:	Project director and lead faculty

Fear of evaluation diminished with the development of the implementation and evaluation plans. Staff gradually saw both instruments as useful tools for them and their staff, not finished products for an external auditor. In fact, staff later said that it was during this period that they came to view me as a staff educator, rather than a project evaluator, and one of the team rather than an outsider. In retrospect, as the projects developed, implementation and evaluation appeared to mesh into a singular way of thinking about planning, conducting and assessing effectiveness of project activities.

THE EVALUATOR AS FACILITATOR

Following the initial planning meeting of all project staff in Spring 1987, I served as a resource to project staff in their individual planning and evaluation activities. I also attended each national meeting of all project staff and made annual one-day visits to each project site during the first few years of the demonstration project.

While the major purpose of the visits to each project site was to assist staff in developing and refining their implementation and evaluation plans, they provided additional benefits. Faculty and college administrators saw me as a representative of the national project, giving those individuals working on the home front a sense of their importance.

Early in the project, this visibility of a national project representative was particularly helpful to project staff at each site who were attempting to generate support and involvement of the faculty. My visits to the project sites often were planned to coincide with local advisory committee meetings so that the members from the participating nursing homes and other agencies could identify with the national effort. At each site, I held work sessions with project staff, met with either the total nursing faculty or groups of faculty involved with project activities, and sometimes presented short evaluation workshops.

Since I was in a professional staff role, rather than an administrative role in the project, and received a consultant fee for these site visits from the host program, staff viewed me as an advisor to, rather than judge of their efforts. They frequently used me as a sounding board for ideas not yet developed into plans and later said that they knew my perspective would be "in" because of my relationship with the two national project leaders. Meeting with individual project staff on their home ground away from the other project personnel also may have contributed to a willingness to share details of problems and conflicts, such as those involving personnel, that they were less likely to discuss with the total group at national staff meetings. Moreover, during the first few years of the demonstration project when the stress level of the conscientious staff at the local project sites was high, the availability of a listener or counselor who had some grasp of the big picture and knew the players was often appreciated. It seemed to help staff deal with challenges inherent in framing their project activities and adjusting from a faculty role to a new role as project director or coordinator. In summary, the site visits served many purposes, while giving me a sense of the uniqueness of each project in contributing to the overall project effort.

At national staff meetings, my role was again that of a resource person and facilitator, guided by the topic at hand. While the agenda for each meeting included a report on evaluation activities for the "umbrella project," I also participated in discussions of each project's current status. At most staff meetings, the agenda scheduled time for each site's project director to report on how her project was progressing and to share problems, strategies and successes. As needed, my role was that of a resource person and facilitator of data-based decision making. During these sessions the group almost naturally shaped a "problem-solving" period at the end of each report, in which project directors from each demonstration site would ask the group for suggestions to deal with a current issue or problem. Since the different projects frequently faced similar problems (i.e., faculty fearful of losing classroom time to gerontology), ideas from other staff were freely shared and often useful.

Attending the national staff meetings also enabled me to acquire a feel for the overall project as well as to keep abreast of trends and common needs. I usually took notes at the meetings, and they were often referred to in planning meetings with the two national project administrators. At one of these planning discussions near the end of the first year of the project, we noted how stressful the first year had been for project staff. They were grappling with completing the implementation and evaluation plans, jump-starting their faculty on gerontology continuing education and curriculum analysis, initiating new relationships with nursing homes and writing that important first annual progress report. At the fall 1988 national staff meeting, I consequently planned an exercise intended both to help them see how much they had learned and accomplished in terms of project administration and to obtain some process evaluation data that could be fed back into ongoing project operation. The one-hour brainstorming exercise entailed project staff identifying, on paper, essential components and practices of effective project administration. The results were shared verbally and then compiled into "A Guide to Successful Project Administration," which recorded for each other as well as others their advice regarding project management, planning, personnel and communication. (The *Guide* is reprinted in Chapter 6.) This process of identifying and sharing what they had learned reinforced effective strategies and boosted the sometimes waning spirits, outcomes as valuable as the product produced.

Also useful was the pattern of using questions as agenda items at each national staff meeting, which took hold about mid-way through the demonstration project. This practice proved effective in two ways. First, the questions helped maintain focus during the always enthusiastic discussions. Second, staff members came to meetings with ideas for responding to the questions, which were usually developed by the two national grant administrators with input from the evaluator. For example, in 1989, with one more year of the demonstration project still to come, the following questions served as a basis for considering whether or not each site was making progress in demonstrating that its approach to changing curriculums and the clinical teaching of gerontological nursing was worth disseminating:

What are the major outcomes of your project?

Can other colleges do the same thing? And if so, why should they?

What outcomes will be the most lasting?

What has been the most difficult for you to accomplish?

What would you do differently?

What outcomes at your site will be the most lasting?

Similarly, at a meeting during the last year of the demonstration project, these types of questions guided the discussions:

What are the major impact areas of your project?

What did you learn about meeting the objectives as the grant moved along?

What took place that prompted or hindered outcomes?

What would you do differently?

What serendipitous findings and insights have you gained while meeting the objectives?

Given what you have learned, what advice would you give to another school to promote change?

The resulting discussion led to an identification and compilation of what the project directors learned, year by year, according to each of the project's objectives. Not only was this information useful in helping each project formulate its final report, it set the stage for the dissemination project, providing a "lessons-learned mind-set" that was invaluable in launching the dissemination project.

THE EVALUATOR AS ASSESSOR

As previously indicated, each project site was responsible for designing and carrying out its individualized Evaluation Plan with modest evaluation funds built into each site's budget for one day's consultation with the evaluator. In addition, funds were budgeted under the national "umbrella project" for the overall evaluation of the collective effort of the six projects. Consequently, I was responsible for conducting the evaluation assessing the common outcome variables related to changes in each program's curriculum, faculty and students. Since each project addressed the same objectives, but each in its own way, the outcome variables for these objectives were the same in each project's Evaluation Plan, allowing for common evaluation tools. With data collection assistance of staff at each site, I designed the instruments assessing these variables and analyzed the data. The instruments that were administered both at the beginning of the project in fall 1987 and again in spring 1990 included the Faculty Attitude Survey, which assessed ADN faculty attitudes toward the role of ADN education in preparing students for employment in long-term care facilities and their attitudes about including gerontological nursing in the ADN curriculum. Faculty also completed standardized instruments assessing knowledge of and attitudes toward aging. The ADN Curriculum Survey assessed the amount of time designated for gerontological nursing in both the classroom and clinical facilities and the preparation of faculty in gerontology. Students in the project programs were also surveyed at entrance and graduation to assess their attitudes toward future employment in longterm care facilities, and they completed instruments designed to assess knowledge of and attitudes toward aging.

Because of the value of the baseline data to the project's planning, summaries of each program's results were distributed to each project director. The overall findings were discussed at national project staff meetings and an executive summary presented to the national advisory committee. Each project also received a final evaluation report, comparing the pre- and post-project findings for the individual program compared to the pooled data from all six project programs.

EVALUATION ROLE CHANGE: FROM DEMONSTRATION TO DISSEMINATION

As indicated thus far in this chronicle of the project's partnership between planning and evaluation, my role during the demonstration phase related as much to planning and facilitating the project effort as it did to assessing the outcomes. When the dissemination phase of the Partnership Project began in fall 1991, a greater proportion of evaluation activities focused on more traditional assessment tasks for the national or "umbrella project." While I attended and participated in the annual staff and national advisory committee meetings, much of my involvement with the project now shifted to designing and conducting the outcome evaluation of the national dissemination phase, whose goal was to influence ADN programs across the country to increase the emphasis of gerontological nursing in their curriculums.

In the dissemination phase, consequently, the scope of evaluation activities expanded from the programs of the original six project sites to all ADN programs in the United States. The project's design outlined a two-pronged, complementary approach to sharing the lessons learned in their successful efforts to change the curriculum. First, each of the six programs targeted other ADN programs in its state and surrounding states to receive specific support services, such as regional workshops and consultation aimed at increasing gerontological nursing content and clinical learning experiences. On the national level, the project planned and sponsored three national conferences co-sponsored by the National League for Nursing; produced a videotape, *Time to Care*; and wrote a curriculum guidebook, *Teaching Gerontology*. Each of these national project activities was aimed at exposing faculty to the rationale and process for increasing the emphasis of gerontological nursing in the curriculum.

The project's purpose and design therefore guided the evaluation plan for the national dissemination phase. Since the intended outcome of the project was an increase in the gerontological nursing content in the curriculum of ADN programs, an outcome study was needed to determine if such changes occurred. Moreover, it would be important to know the participation level and to what extent the national conferences, videotape and curriculum guidebook, as well as regional project activities, were effective in contributing to any changes.

In order to determine the status of gerontological nursing in the ADN curriculum prior to and at the end of the dissemination project, I designed, with input and feedback from project staff, and pre-tested an instrument assessing the type and amount of classroom content and clinical learning experiences that address well, frail and ill elderly adults. Using this instrument, all ADN programs in the United States were surveyed in May 1991 and again in May 1993 to determine if changes in gerontological nursing curriculum content had occurred during the period of the dissemination project. A second questionnaire, which was attached to the May 1993 curriculum questionnaire, assessed the number of ADN faculty participating in the national and regional conferences and workshops and the number who utilized the videotape and curriculum guidebook.

These 1991 and 1993 national data provided the basis for conclusions regarding the effectiveness of the overall project effort in promoting an increase in gerontological nursing in ADN curriculum in the United States. The 1993 survey returns also served as a measure of the number of programs and faculty exposed to the project's message and obtained an assessment of the value of each major project activity in promoting curriculum changes. Furthermore, using this national database, I extrapolated data from the ADN programs targeted by each of the six projects and summarized findings so that each project would have an evaluation of its particular dissemination effort.

In addition to this evaluation report based upon responses to the national survey from programs targeted by its regional effort, each of the six projects also conducted its own complimentary dissemination evaluation, part of which incorporated the same evaluation criteria used in the national survey. The five evaluation criteria, developed by the evaluator following discussions at an early 1991 project staff meeting, provided a basis for both planning and evaluating dissemination activities. They are:

1. Provide rationale for incorporating gerontological nursing in the ADN curriculum.
2. Provide rationale for incorporating long-term care clinical learning in the ADN curriculum.
3. Provide information on the process for undertaking changes to increase gerontological nursing in the ADN curriculum.
4. Promote faculty support for changes to increase gerontological nursing in the ADN curriculum.
5. Help prepare faculty for teaching role in long-term care settings.

The term *criteria* was chosen to emphasize their importance in planning and prioritizing dissemination activities, and to indicate their later use in evaluating the process, as opposed to the outcome of the activities. (The outcome measure, as noted previously, was the amount of gerontological nursing content and clinical learning experiences in ADN programs.) These criteria consequently served as the basis for evaluating the contribution of each dissemination activity to curriculum change and were used in both the 1993 national survey and in each project's evaluation of its regional activities (conferences, workshops and consultation services).

Another main evaluation responsibility during the dissemination phase focused on the videotape, *Time to Care*, which received separate evaluation attention soon after its production in spring 1991. The video was the first major product of the dissemination effort and would serve to draw national attention to other dissemination activities. I therefore designed a tool to assess its effectiveness in accomplishing its purposes (to provide a rationale for incorporating nursing home clinical teaching in the ADN curriculum and give examples of What and How students learn in the nursing home) and to obtain information about its potential future use. The questionnaire consequently included an item asking respondents, after viewing the video, to indicate which types of identified audiences they thought would benefit from the video.

The methodology for the video evaluation consisted of administering the brief questionnaire to individuals attending one of 14 conferences conducted by faculty and staff of the six project programs during May and June of 1991 prior to and immediately following screenings of the video. ADN students enrolled in two Partnership programs also viewed the video and completed the questionnaire as part of a classroom experience before their first clinical experience in a nursing home. As with all evaluation studies in the project, findings were presented at project staff and national advisory committee meetings and reports published in the quarterly newsletter of the project. (See Appendix B.)

LESSONS LEARNED ABOUT EVALUATION

1. Probably the most critical factor to the effective use of a project evaluator is continued involvement with the project from the planning stages to the preparation of the final report. General evaluation plans outlined in the grant application must be at least reviewed by the proposed evaluator, and familiarity with the overall design is necessary so that the evaluator is an informed, willing participant.

2. The evaluator should have a philosophy of evaluation that links planning and evaluation. When evaluation principles and strategies are incorporated into initial and ongoing decision-making and priority-setting, project planning is enhanced by clarity of focus, project implementation is guided by concrete landmarks and project evaluation is simplified.

3. Build in ongoing participation of the evaluator in project staff meetings or use other methods to maintain visibility of evaluation throughout the project. Involvement of the evaluator in staff meetings benefits both the evaluator, by keeping him or her informed and available to contribute to project development as well as evaluation, and benefits project staff, who can be encouraged to use evaluation as a tool for making planning decisions. Use strategies that establish the evaluator as part of the group rather than an outsider.

4. Select a project evaluator who has at least some familiarity with the discipline on which the project focuses so that goals and objectives can be interpreted and operationalized for use in instruments developed to measure outcome variables. Also valuable is flexibility and creativity, along with a willingness to work with

project principals in designing evaluation tools. A research purist's orientation to measurement and quantitative outcome evaluation would likely restrict the involvement of project staff in evaluation and could limit the type and amount of useful information fed back into project development.

5. The benefits of a close working relationship between the evaluator and the project administrators were evident in this project. While this close relationship may not always be possible, frequent communication and involvement of the evaluator as a member of the staff will promote such a relationship and benefit the project.

REFERENCES

Council on Foundations (1993a). A model for foundation programs: The Kellogg approach to evaluating clusters of grants, In *Evaluation for foundations: Concepts, cases, guidelines, resources.* (p. 232). San Francisco: Jossey-Bass.

Council on Foundations (1993b). Evaluation as a creative key to institutional change: The Winthrop Rockefeller Foundation's at-risk youth grant program for schools. In *Evaluation for foundations: Concepts, cases, guidelines, resources.* (p. 232). San Francisco: Jossey-Bass.

Hanson, H. A. (1994a). Changes in gerontological curriculum content and clinical learning experiences 1990–1993. *Newslink.*

Hanson, H. A. (1994b). Evaluation highlights: The community college-nursing home project. *Newslink.*

Hanson, H. A., & Waters, V. (1991). The sequence of curriculum change in gerontology: Faculty first. *Nursing & Health Care, 12*(10), 516–519.

6

Leadership and Educational Change

In the preface of this book, I suggested that our story of the community college-nursing home partnership might help others who are setting up a structure for a grant-funded project, or who are thinking about strategies for changing a curriculum, or who see faculty in need of help with changing roles and teaching practices. Now in this summary, my advice will appear paradoxical: the process of leading a faculty group into new territory is more about not knowing than knowing. The secret is in searching for the answers, not in the answers themselves.

As nurses we are magnetically attracted to certainty. There are surely good explanations for our discomfort with ambiguity, both historical and sociological, but continuing to act as though there is always or almost always one right answer handicaps us now more than ever. A struggle between ambiguity and certainty is tellingly played out in nursing education where an earnest desire to graduate nurses who think critically and independently is often vitiated by teaching practices based on complying with authority and extolling factual knowledge. As American society becomes increasingly diverse and health care issues more complex, the traditional approaches to basic and continuing education come up short. Educational leadership today faces a daunting task: to facilitate the learning of unknown students who will care in the unknown tomorrows for unknown clients in unknown ways. The recent past particularly suggests to us that the only prediction about the future in health care delivery that will hold true is that no predictions will hold true. It is a time for fresh imaginings.

A new and higher level of leadership is called for, stressing community and collaboration relationships, and focusing on real change in the way education for nursing is thought about and practiced. Education is not, as it was defined by President Garfield in the last century, Mark Hopkins on one end of a bench and a student on the other, but it is instead a complex network of people who contribute to, become part of, and are affected by an assemblage of teaching/learning experiences.

More than twenty years ago, in the middle of a consultation that was going very very badly, I was struck by what was, for me, a revelation. The faculty group was simmering with old anger and I, the consultant, stumbled around, grasping for verbal footing. As my feelings of desperation intensified, a new insight flooded my mind: I am not the only person in this room responsible for what happens. In the wake of that situation, which changed for the better when my interactions with the group moved to a new premise, I saw leadership in a new light. I began to practice new ways of being a group leader. The Community College-Nursing Home Partnership project, because of its scope and structure, provided an especially interesting opportunity to consciously elect certain actions and responses, and to reflect on consequences of those actions.

From the beginning a principal challenge lay in resisting telling people what to do. By the time the project staff was fully formed, there had been months of proposal development and a year of planning which had involved, other than Susan Sherman and me, only selected faculty at Ohlone and CCP. The program directors and faculty who would work on project activities from the other four schools expected quite reasonably to be given direction from me as the project administrator, and, certainly, after more than a year of thinking and talking about the project, I had formulated hopes and expectations. Nonetheless I knew it was important to help new projects get started without telling them how to start. At the first meeting of the full project staff in April 1987 the major topic on the agenda for the two-day session was to think and talk with each other about all the activities that *could* or *might* be undertaken at each site to fulfill the project purposes. The discussion was rich with possibilities, but members of the group were frustrated; frustration was expressed then, and remembered in detail in a later discussion. There seemed to be too many ideas, and no order among them. Members of the group did not want the session to end without some plan for what to do when they returned home and they pushed for a discussion about what to do first. With some enthusiasm a concensus decision was made that the first order of business at each site would be to conduct an assessment of the educational needs of faculty and nursing home staff for new information about gerontology and long term care.

At the last staff meeting, held six years later, that first meeting was still vivid in staff member minds. We were reviewing the project, identifying those parts of it that seemed to have worked well, and those not so well. Along with the frustration, people remembered feeling satisfied by the discussion about where to start, and enthusiastic about the concensus decision that had been reached. Some had noted my nondirective approach as discussion leader and had watched as well as participated in the group process as it moved toward a satisfying conclusion.

On the other side of the coin, it was not easy for me to refrain from stepping in when people seemed not to know what they were doing, or when they were going in directions that seemed mistaken. I had to remind myself that the important value is not control, but connectedness. The leader's job is not to hold things together; it is to create an atmosphere in which the appropriate controls will emerge as the group establishes itself and takes up its task. I wanted us to work with each other in such a way that we could trust in the unfolding of order. The group became self-monitoring in a voluntary, affirming fashion. Strong peer relationships emerged between people who had not known each other previously and who lived in different parts of the country, carried out in occasional face-to-face meetings and frequent telephone exchanges.

A leader has no greater responsibility than that those led benefit and grow personally as a result of the leader's actions. Earlier I mentioned feeling a particular attachment to the goal of faculty development as part of any funded project in associate degree education. I believe that the project should be written, funded, and managed in such a way that each member of the faculty has a chance to be enriched and offered new opportunities to learn, to expand horizons, to gain a new or larger perspective, and to develop new skills. Neither work loads nor institutional expectations foster community college faculty involvement in scholarly pursuits or other professional activities. The time and added resources brought to a faculty in an extramurally-funded project should provide opportunities to do so.

As part of the national project, Susan Sherman, Helen Hanson, and I put emphasis on helping project principals develop new skills and become more effective as nurse educators. Helen Hanson coached faculty groups at each demonstration site, at national meetings of project principals, and in meetings with individuals, helping them think through relationships among intended outcomes, implementation activities, and assessment methods. A training session with organizational development consultants was scheduled when the project purposes changed from demonstration to dissemination. Staff meetings for project principals were planned to include time for what might be called group problem-solving. In these sessions and others the intent was to provide leadership which did not direct, but made self-direction possible, which gave feedback but did not criticize, which trusted and promoted trust.

The ultimate success of our project depended upon the effectiveness of the six demonstration projects, and thereby we saw a national interest in supporting and enhancing the leadership abilities of project principals. At Helen Hanson's instigation, a staff session early in the second year of the project (October 1988) was devoted to a discussion of the qualities and characteristics of leadership that foster success in an educational change project. As she relates in Chapter 5, the purpose of the discussion was twofold: to affirm how well they were doing in new leadership roles, and to enunciate and share ideas about leadership that might prompt continued growth and improvement. Dr. Hanson summarized the essence of the discussion, and the summary was distributed as a guide to successful project administration.

It could be said with some justification that the characteristics and behaviors listed by the staff of the project in 1988 did become guidelines for action. As I reviewed minutes covering six years of meetings, annual reports, and end-of-project comments from project staff members about their experience, it struck me that much of what has gone on is an elaboration of the guide to project administration laid down in that earlier discussion. Given our desire in this publication to highlight what seemed to work well for our project, the 1988 guide to managing educational change is reprinted here. It provides a useful summary of major points in the preceding chapters.

A GUIDE TO SUCCESSFUL PROJECT ADMINISTRATION*

People

- Pull in, create, or otherwise procure creative, compulsive, bright, enthusiastic people who enjoy challenge/growth and can tolerate ambiguity.

---

*Based on a staff discussion on October 19, 1988; Helen A. Hanson, Evaluation Consultant, took minutes and prepared this summary of the discussion.

- Get a geriatric nurse practitioner to help with project activities, especially faculty and staff development.
- Identify key leaders, then delegate and trust in them.
- Have a stable and capable faculty who basically care about one another.

Planning

- Begin with a well-developed, communicated plan.
- Allocate designated and budgeted time for project administration—then double it.
- Establish an advisory board early and involve and engage the members in meaningful participation.
- Set clear priorities on a routine basis and adjust expectations so that success is guaranteed.
- Spend more time in planning. At planning meetings, have some ideas in reserve.
- Define and prioritize the responsibilities of the project staff.
- Use implementation and evaluation plans to guide and define project activities and set priorities. Review project goals in a systematic way at regular intervals to keep on track.
- Plan project activities that will get nursing home staff and community members on campus to strengthen their identification with the college.
- Never plan a program for others without including them in the planning.
- Expect everything to take longer than you think it should.

Communication

- Listen to faculty and clinical agency staff. Value their input.
- Quickly make the project visible to faculty; share a high profile of the project with the faculty.
- Keep faculty and agency staff informed, verbally and in writing, of all project activities, not just those that directly affect them.

- Hold weekly meetings with project staff and monthly meetings with faculty and with nursing home staff and DONs; prepare agenda and distribute minutes.
- Prepare and regularly distribute calendars of project events.
- Problem solve openly.
- Recognize and praise each accomplishment, not just the big activities.

Personnel Management

- Put competent people in staff training roles; replace staff who are unhappy.
- Involve as many faculty as possible on various aspects of the project.
- Build a team; have all segments of faculty and cross-section of the curriculum committee represented.
- Involve all faculty members in the project in some way and promote ownership by all. Accept all levels of involvement by faculty, but expect that there will be some faculty who never buy into the project.
- Recognize that there is always resistance to change and that change takes time. Use change strategies that have been successful in the past. Don't be threatened by resistance but use that energy in a positive way.
- Keep people focused on the task; in committees do the "scut work" yourself and give others the more glamorous tasks.
- Never dismiss any idea in a brainstorming session. Value every participant for contributing. "Stroke" often.
- Create a true partnership with the faculty. Don't just do *to*.
- Balance the work groups with three quarters of the group made up of people who are already committed to the project and one quarter of people you would like to be committed.
- Form small committees that have responsibility for a defined part of the project and a defined time limit.
- Try to provide some incentives and rewards (money, release time, public recognition) to faculty and clinical agency staff who work on the project.
- Look on the diverseness of faculty and nursing home personnel as an asset to be used in meeting the objectives of the project.

- Foster the formation of strong relationships between clinical faculty and nursing home staff. Recognize that both faculty and nursing home staff will fear the unknown.
- Do not pass judgment on the capabilities of nursing home partners before you get to know them.

Project Management

- Learn the budget system quickly and well, and computerize budget.
- Turn budget operation and paperwork over to secretary.
- Meet with your superior on a regular basis and review achievements before addressing problems and new challenges.
- Maintain a record of all project activities with dates and log the project's decision-making processes.
- Develop protocols (schedule of preparatory activities) for common types of project activities (e.g., continuing education programs).
- Support project-related activities in small ways even if not personally involved in them.
- When appropriate, run meetings with a co-leader, with one person focusing on the agenda and the other on process.
- Do not try to do a full-time job in a half-time position. Learn to say "No" and not feel guilty. Recognize that there is more work to do than there is time and there will be no real feelings of completion. Control the number of committees you serve on.
- Be prepared to accept some setbacks and frustrations. Develop a support system that includes people from both service and education.
- Begin contacts with a new affiliating agency by going to the top administrators first and gaining their support.
- Network with nursing home administrators and DONs by going to lunch or dinner with them.
- Get partners to invest some ownership in the project: Encourage some monetary or other material investment.
- Join the local "power group."
- Formalize the informal network by establishing regular, brief meeting times.
- Maintain good health and a sense of humor.

- Do not expect too much too soon. Accept that change is never or rarely dramatic, but incremental. Faculty enlightenment comes not as an apocalypse, but as a slow dawn. You rarely see it happen but usually know that it has occurred.

HOW THIS BOOK WAS "NAMED"

About the title of this book, *The Narrative Enlarging*: it derives from a lengthy description of a dinner table scene in Virginia Woolf's novel, *To the Lighthouse*. At the beginning of the meal the central character, a woman, "saw things truly. . . . They all sat separate. Nothing seemed to have merged." She knows that it is up to her to begin the "merging and flowing and creating," and as the dinner progresses their stories interrupt, entwine and join, the narrative enlarging until "some change went through them all. . . . they had their common cause against the fluidity outside" (Woolf, 1927, pp. 126, 147). This book took shape in the hope that it would make a contribution to enlarging the narrative, specifically the narrative which advances nurses in understanding and responding to the care needs of the frail elderly, but more generally the narrative which emboldens nurse educators to change, to embrace a broader vision, and to see the whole community as the classroom.

REFERENCE

Woolf, V. (1927). *To the lighthouse*. New York: Harcourt, Brace & World.

Appendix A
1985 and 1989 Project Proposals

PROJECT PROPOSAL
(Abridged & Revised 9/1/86)

THE COMMUNITY COLLEGE-NURSING HOME
PARTNERSHIP: IMPROVING CARE
THROUGH EDUCATION

Ohlone College — Fremont, California
Community College of Philadelphia, Pennsylvania

Funded by the W. K. Kellogg Foundation

Funding Years 1986–1990

BACKGROUND

Between now and the year 2000, health care providers face what has been called "the demographic imperative": a continuing increase in number of persons over 65, with tripling of the number of those over 85. Nursing home beds will nearly double by the year 2000. This project proposes to show how 772 associate degree nursing programs, dispersed widely through urban and rural America, could influence present and future care in the 23,600 nursing homes in this country.*

Nursing potential in the nation's nursing homes can be richly enhanced through the development by associate degree nursing faculty and students of a teaching-learning mission and environment within the nursing home. With population and life span data pointing to increasing numbers of the frail and dependent aged, anticipatory action on the part of

---

* In funding this project, the W. K. Kellogg Foundation urged a wider scope. The approval letter from Dr. Helen Grace, Program Director, added this charge: "And finally, while the major thrust of your proposal is toward improvement of care in nursing homes, the linkage of community colleges to the broader realm of care of the elderly, both in long term care facilities as well as those in other community based settings and homes, is of interest to us. We would trust that as the project develops these linkages might be expanded to extend beyond the nursing component of community colleges to other areas of study and beyond nursing homes to broader based community settings."

nursing educators is clearly called for. The system of associate degree nursing education, imbedded in the structure of communities across this nation, is well positioned to take on this challenge. Demonstration centers in three regions (South, Northeast, and West), will allow project outcomes to be generalized to the country as a whole.

MAJOR PURPOSES*

1. Develop nursing potential in nursing homes, through inservice education for staff at all levels, to enhance quality of care being delivered, and to establish active teaching centers for nursing education.
2. Demonstrate and influence the redirection of associate degree nursing education to encompass active preparation for nursing roles in long-term care organizations as well as acute general hospitals.

SPECIFIC OBJECTIVES

1. Establish mechanisms that foster communication between associate degree nursing programs and nursing homes, and develop cooperative activities aimed at improving the quality of patient care.
2. Develop structure and incentive for faculty development activities to stimulate interest in and acquire skills for assisting nursing home personnel in upgrading care.
3. Conduct curriculum study, experimentation, and evaluation to identify and describe curriculum changes necessary to increase program emphasis on gerontologic nursing.
4. Design learning experiences to foster in students positive attitudes toward work with old people, and to encourage graduate interest in gerontologic nursing as a career choice.
5. Evaluate all project activities, both process and outcomes.

---

* As indicated in the footnote on page 84, a third major purpose has been added at the request of the W. K. Kellogg Foundation. Project objectives, method and activities are being enlarged to encompass this third broader purpose.

6. Develop plans for dissemination of findings to associate degree nursing educators, nursing homes, and other nurses working in the long-term care field.

GENERAL METHOD

Six community colleges in different parts of the nation will each work with 1–4 nursing homes to accomplish the purposes and objectives of this project, thereby demonstrating a model for associate degree nursing programs and nursing homes in general. Within each of the six demonstration units (one associate degree program and 1–4 nursing homes in the college's service area), a set of activities will be planned and implemented to achieve objectives 1 through 5. Geographic diversity of demonstration sites will permit generalizing about outcomes and strengthen the impact of the demonstration on other programs and nursing homes. The project administrative structure is designed to assure close supervision of each demonstration site while providing for strong communication links between and among all projects. A national advisory committee, composed of representatives from several disciplines and groups working in the arena of geriatrics and gerontology, will review project goals and dilemmas (as they develop) and provide direction. Evaluation activities and planning for dissemination of project outcomes to the general audience of associate degree educators and nursing home personnel will be the responsibility of the project administrative group.

Project management is designed to provide control of demonstration site activities together with extensive sharing of information among project participants, yielding an account of project experiences which will be of considerable use in realizing the two overall purposes of this ambitious project.

PROJECT MANAGEMENT

Overall project management is located at Ohlone College. Project administrator is Verle Waters, with two regional project directors: Sharlene Limon, also located at Ohlone College, is Project Director, West, and Susan Sherman, Community College of Philadelphia is Project Director, East. The project administrator and regional directors serve as the administrative unit responsible for all project activities.

The advisory board will meet four times in the project period. As of September 3, 1986, members of the advisory committee are:

Genrose J. Alfano, R.N., Editor, GERIATRIC NURSING, American Journal of Care for the Aging

Richard Besdine, M.D., Director, Travellers Center on Aging, University of Connecticut, Farmington, CT

H. Terri Brower, Ed.D., F.A.A.N., Dean and Professor, Auburn University School of Nursing, Auburn University, AL

Ann Burack-Weiss, M.S.S.W., Training Consultant, Brookdale Institute on Aging and Adult Human Development, Columbia University, New York, NY

Geraldine Evans, Ph.D., President, Rochester Community College, Rochester, MN

Barry Gurland, M.D., Director, The Center for Geriatrics and Gerontology, New York, NY

Lillian L. Hamilton, R.N., M.P.A., Executive Director, Care America Foundation, Nashville, TN

Lucille Joel, Ed.D., F.A.A.N., Professor and Director for Clinical Affairs, Rutgers University College of Nursing, Newark, NJ

Diane Mancino, M.A., R.N., Director of Programs, National Student Nurses' Association, New York, NY

James McCall, Director, Organizational Services, Ross Laboratories, Columbus, OH

Ken F. Oldham, Education Specialist, Beverly Foundation, Pasadena, CA

Robert E. Parilla, Ph.D., President, Montgomery College, Rockville, MD

Leopold Selker, Ph.D., Assistant to the President for the Houston Center and Professor, Texas Woman's University, Houston, TX

Sharon Simson, Ph.D., Associate Chief, Geriatrics and Associate Professor, Department of Mental Health Sciences, Hahnemann University, Philadelphia, PA

Norma S. Tucker, Ed.D., Associate Dean for Continuing Education and Community Development, Dundalk Community College, Baltimore, MD

In addition, the American Association of Retired Persons and the American Health Care Association have agreed to designate a representative of each organization to serve on the committee.

ACTIVITIES TO ACHIEVE PROJECT OBJECTIVES

Objective 1.

Establish mechanisms that foster communication between associate degree nursing programs and nursing homes, and develop cooperative activities aimed at improving the quality of patient care.

Activities to achieve this objective:

1.1   Identify six colleges for participation in this project.

      1.1.1.   Four colleges have been selected, in addition to Ohlone College and the Community College of Philadelphia; Valencia Community College in Orlando, Florida; Triton College in River Grove, Illinois; Weber State College in Ogden, Utah; and Shoreline Community College in Seattle, Washington.

      The selection of participating community colleges was based, in part, on the following criteria:

      a.   History of successful relationships with clinical agencies and nursing service personnel.

      b.   Faculty support of project activities.

      c.   National League for Nursing Accreditation.

      d.   Ability to enlist the participation of 1–4 nursing homes.

      e.   Indication of previous successful effort to include gerontologic nursing content.

      f.   Institutional commitment to continue project activities once funding period is over.

1.2   Initiate relationships with nursing homes in the areas where participating colleges are located. Faculty in participating colleges will establish a working relationship with 1–4 nursing homes, gaining the participation of the nursing home staff.

1.3   Nursing faculty, working with and through licensed staff of the nursing home, including the designated inservice instructor, will assist with staff development for all levels of personnel.

1.4   Selected staff in project nursing homes will participate in inter-project meetings to examine common problems and share solutions and strategies.

Objective 2.

Develop structure and incentive for faculty development activities to stimulate interest in and acquire skills for assisting nursing home personnel in upgrading care.

2.1   Develop short courses and workshops for faculty on gerontology topics. Major resources in each region will be engaged to assist with this important undertaking.

2.2   Provide released time for nursing faculty to pursue activities related to grant activities. (Examples: lead curriculum revision, enroll in graduate or continuing education courses, or work in a participating nursing home.)

2.3   Provide opportunity for faculty in project colleges to meet and work together on problems of mutual concern.

Objective 3.

Conduct curriculum study, experimentation, and evaluation to identify and describe changes necessary to increase emphasis on gerontologic nursing.

3.1   Identify graduate competencies in the field of gerontologic nursing appropriate to the ADN curriculum.

3.2   Specify objectives, length and type of clinical experience with elderly patients needed in an ADN program to achieve those competencies.

3.3   Describe overall curriculum adjustments in ADN curriculum to accommodate greater emphasis on nursing homes.

Objective 4.

Design learning experiences to foster in students positive attitudes toward work with old people and to encourage graduate interest in gerontologic nursing as a career choice.

Objective 5.

Evaluate all project activities, both process and outcomes. Specific measures will be used to measure insofar as possible:

5.1   Baseline perceptions of nursing home staff toward the care they give and toward their patients.

5.2   Perceived impact of project activities on level of patient care in participating nursing homes.

5.3   Effect of project activities on employee satisfaction, absentee rate, and turnover in participating nursing homes.

5.4   Changes in curriculum introduced by nursing faculty to meet identified gerontologic nursing competencies.

5.5   Changes in job-seeking behavior of graduates of modified ADN curricula.

5.6   Changes in student and faculty attitudes toward care of the frail, dependent, elderly patient.

Objective 6.

Develop plans for dissemination of findings to nursing education and nursing homes.

FUNDING STRUCTURE

The total budget request for this project is $2,267,550 with the request that the Foundation makes grants to six separate participating institutions. The budget reflects the following categories:

1. Personnel for project administration and direction
2. Faculty development
3. Nursing home staff development
4. Equipment, supplies, postage, telephone
5. Interproject and advisory committee travel
6. Evaluation

Ohlone College provides overall leadership and direction for this project, including monitoring the achievement of objectives and grant management in participating institutions.

PROJECT PROPOSAL
(Abridged and Revised 6/7/90)

DISSEMINATION: EXPANDING COLLABORATION BETWEEN COMMUNITY COLLEGES AND NURSING HOMES

Funded by the W. K. Kellogg Foundation
Funding Years: 1990–1993

BACKGROUND

For the four year period 1986–1990, the W. K. Kellogg Foundation funded Ohlone College, Fremont, CA, the Community College of Philadelphia, and four additional colleges to conduct a multi-site demonstration project entitled "The Community College-Nursing Home Partnership: Improving Care Through Education." Dissemination of lessons learned, insights gained and models for collaboration developed through demonstration project activities is now proposed. The two overall purposes of the demonstration project now drawing to a close have been achieved at the six demonstration sites through a variety of activities. Those purposes are:

1. to develop nursing potential in long-term care settings through in-service education, and
2. to influence the redirection of associate degree nursing education to include active preparation for nursing roles in long-term care settings.

There is reason to believe that the successful experiences mounted at each of the demonstration sites can be, and to some extent are being, adopted at other community colleges and in other nursing homes. This proposal for funding of a dissemination project will describe purposes, objectives and detailed activities to extend the demonstration site achievements.

PURPOSES

The four major purposes for this dissemination project are to:

1. Develop dissemination resource materials, including a videotape and curriculum handbook.

2. Provide conferences, workshops, and consultation at six regional centers to share strategies and skills with Associate Degree Nursing educators and nursing home personnel.

3. Collaborate with other organizations, including regional Geriatric Education Centers (GECs), the National League for Nursing (NLN), the American Nurses Association (ANA), the National Gerontological Nursing Association (NGNA), the American Society of Allied Health Professionals (ASAHP), the American Association of Community and Junior Colleges (AACJC), the American Health Care Association (AHCA), and the American Association of Homes for the Aging (AAHA), in conference and workshop programming which draws upon and extends demonstration site experiences.

4. Monitor and influence, insofar as possible, changing patterns in NCLEX-RN examination, state rules and regulations governing nursing curricula, evolving competency statements from NLN education councils and changing accreditation criteria in relationship to the redirection of Associate Degree Nursing curriculum.

RATIONALE

The major outcomes of the four-year demonstration project can be summarized in three categories:

- curriculum
- faculty
- the nursing home.

The current project staff has reviewed the achievements and experiences of the past four years within these categories, and looked at the implications of demonstration project outcomes for the dissemination project agenda.

Curriculum

Objective Three of the demonstration project, "Conduct curriculum study, experimentation and evaluation to identify and describe curriculum changes necessary to increase program emphasis on geriatric nursing," has been met at each of the six demonstration sites, yielding six different successful curriculum models for associate degree programs. Review of nursing literature at the beginning of our project found, somewhat remarkably, that curriculum models for inclusion of gerontologic content existed for graduate, baccalaureate, diploma and practical nurse education, but there were no references for associate degree curriculum planners. In the course of the demonstration project, literature contributions have begun, and others are in progress. A major dissemination need (and potential) exists for widespread distribution of the six successful curriculum models developed at the demonstration sites. Each site has taken a different approach, and as a whole the experience of changing six programs yields useful and generalizable information about:

- integrating gerontologic concepts throughout the curriculum,
- identifying nursing content most effectively taught through clinical experience in the nursing home,
- defining content needed for staff nurse functions in the nursing home,
- sequencing and placing of specialized gerontologic content in the ADN curriculum,
- selecting of effective teaching-learning methods.

Faculty

Objective Two of the demonstration project proposal, "Develop structure and incentive for the nursing faculty development activities to stimulate interest in and acquire skills for assisting nursing home personnel in upgrading care," combined faculty development and nursing home staff development. In actuality, activities mounted in each demonstration site to accomplish this objective have fallen into three types: some activities have been directed to faculty development, some to staff development in the nursing home, and some have included both groups and served the combined objective. We have learned that faculty development is a central issue in achieving curriculum change to redirect associate degree nursing education. And, that the challenge is complex. In general, nursing faculty values, as well as curriculum decisions, embrace an acute care nursing culture. The wisdom gained through demonstration project activities provides insight and direction for working with faculty groups to achieve a new perspective on curriculum values and choices.

The Nursing Home

Colleges and nursing homes are unaccustomed partners. The nursing home and its employees are isolated from the mainstream of health services and the education of health professionals. Nursing faculty associate primarily with other faculty and with nurses who work in acute care, both of whom hold stereotypical views of long-term care nurses and nursing homes. We have learned how to bridge the communication barriers, how to foster the articulation of mutual goals, and how to work together.

The first of the two major purposes of the demonstration project addressed the development of nursing potential in the nursing home, and demonstration site activities have reflected that commitment. We have learned a great deal about the environments of work and patient care in the nursing home, and have determined with certainty through our own experiences that:

- an educational affiliation between a community college and a nursing home can be positive, and when it is, it impacts favorably on the nursing home environment, and
- clinical education in the nursing home can be successful, and when it is, it enhances nursing education for both students and faculty.

Dissemination activities will target key personnel in the nursing home hierarchy, utilizing knowledge gained through our experiences in working with Directors of Nursing, Staff Development directors, licensed staff, and the certified nursing assistants.

A research study using the Delphi method conducted in the third year of the demonstration project has identified the conditions and qualities of a successful nursing home-college affiliation. These findings offer a solid base for dissemination activities.

ORGANIZATIONAL STRUCTURE AND MANAGEMENT OF DISSEMINATION PROJECT

The Community College of Philadelphia will provide overall project management and leadership. The Project Administrator will be Susan Sherman, Head of the ADN program at CCP, and Project Director—

East for the demonstration project. Verle Waters will serve as Dissemination Project Consultant.

Regional Dissemination Centers (RDCs) will be established at Community College of Philadelphia; Ohlone College, California; Shoreline Community College, Washington; Triton College, Illinois; Weber State College, Utah and Valencia Community College, Florida.

Project Directors will be designated at each of the Regional Dissemination Centers. (In every case, project directors for dissemination will be individuals who have held active roles in the Demonstration Project.) A Project Management Committee, chaired by the Project Administrator and consisting of the Project Consultant and Project Directors from each RDC will provide overall leadership and coordination of dissemination activities.

A National Advisory Committee of ten members will be appointed, and will be convened once each year during the three-year project. An active interdisciplinary committee for the Demonstration Project has provided valuable guidance, and represented Project interests in external groups. It is assumed that several key members of the Demonstration Project Advisory Committee will continue to serve for the Dissemination Project. The Committee will again represent groups important for wider communication of Project activities. Representation from the following groups is proposed: National League for Nursing, American Nurses Association, regional Geriatric Education Centers, American Gerontological Nurses Association, American Society of Allied Health Professionals, American Association of Community and Junior Colleges, American Health Care Association, American Association of Homes for the Aging.

Appendix B
H. Hanson Evaluation Reports

HIGHLIGHTS OF NATIONAL SURVEY

Gerontological Nursing in the ADN Curriculum*

Helen A. Hanson, PhD, RN
Evaluation Consultant, The Community College-Nursing
Home Partnership Project

In the summer of 1991, The Community College-Nursing Home Partnership Project surveyed all 801 ADN programs in the United States to identify the ways that ADN students are being prepared to care for elderly clients. The information obtained from this survey will serve as baseline data for a repeat survey in 1993 that will determine curricular changes that may occur in the interim. The following highlights of the findings from 86 percent of the programs surveyed provide a profile of gerontological nursing in the ADN curriculum as of the 1990–91 academic year. These findings raise important questions about how ADN educators are incorporating nursing care of the elderly in their curriculums. This summary should be useful in stimulating discussions among faculty regarding what, how, and where they might place learning experiences focusing on care of well, frail and ill elderly clients.

Clinical Learning Experiences That Focus on Ill or Frail Elderly Adults

- *Sixty-six percent of the programs provide a nursing home experience in the first year of the program and 20 percent include one in the second year of the curriculum. Twelve percent of the programs have clinical placements in a nursing home in both the first and second year of the curriculum.*

- *First-year nursing home experiences range from one to 44 days in length, with an average of nine days and a median of eight days. The proportion of programs reporting clinical rotations for all students in the first year is:*

---

* First published in the Community College-Nursing Home Project newsletter, *Newslink*, Winter 1992.

None   34%

Less than 6 days   19%

6–12 days   30%

More than 12 days 17%

- *Second-year nursing home placements range from one-half to 30 days, with an average of seven days and a median of six days. The proportion of programs reporting clinical rotations for all students in the second year is:*

None   80%

Less than 6 days   9%

6–12 days   9%

More than 12 days 2%

- *Students in 27 percent of the programs have clinical learning experiences that focus on the ill or frail elderly in long-term care settings other than nursing homes, such as extended care facilities, rehabilitation and mental health facilities, and day care settings.*

- *While 74 percent of the programs report that each student has at least a one-day learning experience in the nursing home, 19 percent of the programs do not use either a nursing home or other long-term care facility to teach nursing care of the ill or frail elderly.*

Clinical or Field Experiences That Focus on Well Elderly Adults

- *Thirty-two percent of the programs provide clinical or field experiences that focus on well elderly adults.*

- *Day care centers are the most frequently used setting for well elderly experiences, where 15 percent of programs report placements. The length of the experience is from two to 48 hours, with an average of eight hours and a median of six hours.*

- *The next most frequently used setting for a well elderly experience is the private home of an older adult. Six percent of programs report such experiences of one to 24 hours in length, with an average of five hours and a median of four hours.*

- *Fewer than four percent of the programs report clinical or field experiences in each of the following other well-elderly settings: nursing homes, retirement centers, nutrition or other clinics, home health agencies and other community settings.*

Classroom Hours Addressing Gerontological Content Areas

- The amount of classroom time allocated to gerontological content ranges from zero to 116 hours, with an average of 16 hours and a median of 11 hours allotted to twelve identified content areas.

- The content area, Common Health Problems of Aging and Nursing Interventions receives the greatest amount of classroom time (an average of almost five hours), followed by Nursing Process as Applied to the Elderly Client (almost three hours). Next is Normal Physical Changes of Aging, which receives an average of two and one-third hours.

- The following content areas each receive an average of one to two hours of classroom time: Normal Psychological Changes of Aging, Attitudes toward Aging, Socio-Cultural Aspects of Aging, Legal/Ethical Issues of Aging, and the Nursing Home Setting.

- Less than one hour of classroom time is typically designated for Community Resources for the Elderly, Demographics of Aging, Theories of Aging, and Politics of Aging.

EVALUATION HIGHLIGHTS

THE COMMUNITY COLLEGE-NURSING HOME PROJECT

Helen A. Hanson, PhD, RN
Evaluation Consultant

Findings from a national survey of ADN programs reveal the extent to which the activities and materials produced by this Kellogg-sponsored project exposed faculty to the rationale and process for increasing the emphasis of gerontological nursing in the ADN curriculum.

In the dissemination phase of this national project, six ADN programs who had participated in the 1987–90 demonstration phase sought to make an impact on the ADN curriculum by sharing how they had increased gerontological nursing in their curriculums. These six Project programs* targeted a total of 146 ADN programs in their geographical areas to receive specific support services, which included regional workshops, conferences and consultation services. The other major Project activities and products promoted nationally were a videotape, **Time to Care**; a curriculum guidebook, **Teaching Gerontology**; and two national conferences co-sponsored by the National League for Nursing.

As one of two questionnaires designed to assess the impact of the dissemination project on ADN education, the findings of this survey reveal the proportion of programs that participated in or used the major activities and teaching materials produced by the Project. The following highlights summarize responses received from 90 (62 percent) of the targeted regional participants and from 371 (44 percent) of 843 programs in the U.S.

*86 percent of the regional sample and 77 percent of the national sample used the videotape, **Time to Care**.*

*72 percent of the regional sample and 58 percent of the national sample used the curriculum guidebook, **Teaching Gerontology**.*

---

* Community College of Philadelphia, Ohlone College (CA), Shoreline Community College (WA), Triton College (IL), Valencia Community College (FL), and Weber State University (UT).

23 percent of the regional sample and 13 percent of the national sample attended one of the Project's two national conferences on gerontological nursing.

44 percent of the regional sample and 36 percent of the national sample heard a presentation by a project representative at a national meeting.

83 percent of the regional sample and 57 percent of the national sample attended one or more regional workshops or conferences sponsored by one of the six sponsoring programs.

These findings show that the videotape, produced in cooperation with the NLN and distributed free to all ADN programs, was the most widely used product by both samples. The regional respondents were next most likely to have attended a regional conference, and then to have used the curriculum guidebook. While almost one-half of the regional sample had heard a presentation by a Project representative at a national meeting, they were least likely to have attended one of the two national conferences sponsored by the Project. Nationally, respondents were almost as likely to have attended a regional workshop or conference as to have used the curriculum guidebook. They were least likely to have attended one of the national conferences or heard a project representative at a national meeting.

EFFECTIVENESS OF DISSEMINATION ACTIVITIES/PRODUCTS

Respondents to the survey were also asked to rate the extent to which each of the Project activities or products was effective in increasing the emphasis of gerontological nursing in ADN education. As shown in the table below, a large majority of both the regional and national samples rated each of the Project's activities as being either Very or Moderately Useful in contributing to curricular change. Almost nine out of ten of both samples indicated that each activity/product was highly successful in providing rationale for strengthening gerontological nursing and including long-term care clinical learning experiences in the ADN curriculum. At least two-thirds responded that each activity or product also provided useful information regarding the process to increase gerontological nursing in the curriculum, and promoted faculty support for changes. Lastly, the curriculum guidebook was cited as most effective in preparing faculty for teaching roles in long-term care settings.

	Video		Book		National Conference		Session Presentation		Local Workshop	
	Reg	Natl	Reg	Natl	Reg	Natl	Reg	Natl	Reg	Natl
Provide rational for gerontological nursing in ADN curriculum	84%	86%	91%	92%	95%	94%	86%	91%	92%	96%
Provide rationale for LTC clinical learning in ADN curriculum	88%	85%	94%	91%	95%	96%	86%	90%	94%	95%
Provide information on process to increase gerontological nursing in ADN curriculum	64%	71%	87%	86%	86%	90%	83%	84%	85%	91%
Promote faculty support for changes	80%	75%	86%	79%	79%	80%	76%	77%	81%	83%
Help prepare faculty for teaching in LTC settings	59%	61%	93%	85%	68%	77%	52%	66%	72%	77%

In conclusion, the dissemination activities and products of The Community College-Nursing Home Partnership reached a large majority of ADN programs in the country. Program directors and faculty were most likely to have used the Project's videotape and curriculum guidebook and to have attended a regional workshop or conference sponsored by one of the six Project programs. Furthermore, ratings of the value and usefulness of these dissemination efforts support the conclusion that each activity and product accomplished its purpose: to provide the rationale and process for strengthening gerontological nursing in the ADN curriculum. The extent to which these subjective ratings were translated into curriculum change is summarized in a companion report of findings from the second evaluation survey assessing the type and amount of classroom content and clinical learning experiences that address well, frail and ill elderly adults.

CHANGES IN GERONTOLOGICAL CURRICULUM CONTENT* AND CLINICAL LEARNING EXPERIENCES 1990–1993

Helen A. Hanson, PhD, RN
Evaluation Consultant

In 1986, six associate degree programs initiated a challenging project aimed at changing the way nurses were educated to care for older Americans. Through their Community College-Nursing Home Partnership Project, funded by the W. K. Kellogg Foundation, these six geographically dispersed programs demonstrated how educators might bring about such change in their own programs.[1] Given the success of their initial efforts to increase the emphasis of gerontological nursing in the curriculum and prepare faculty for new teaching roles in long-term care settings, in 1990 the six programs[2] mounted a national dissemination effort to share the lessons learned in the demonstration project.

The goal of the 1990–1993 dissemination phase was to improve the teaching of gerontological nursing in ADN programs throughout the country, with intense efforts directed at targeted programs in the regions of the six programs. Evaluation of these dissemination efforts consequently focused on determining to what extent the Project increased the emphasis of gerontological nursing in the associate degree nursing (ADN) curriculum. To measure the effect of the Project's activities on the curriculum, all ADN programs in the United States were surveyed in May 1991 and again in May 1993 to assess the type and amount of classroom content and clinical learning experiences that address well, frail and ill elderly adults.

Findings from these two surveys, summarized below, provide a profile of gerontological nursing in the ADN curriculum at the beginning and at

---

* First published in the Community College-Nursing Home Partnership newsletter, *Newslink*, Winter 1994.

[1] Hanson, H. A., & Waters, V. (1991) The Sequence of Curriculum change in Gerontology: Faculty First. *Nursing and Health Care*, 12(10), 516–519.

[2] Community College of Philadelphia, Ohlone College (CA), Shoreline Community College (WA), Triton College (IL), Valencia Community College (FL), & Weber State University (UT).

the end of the dissemination project. They reveal curriculum changes that occurred in the programs that were targeted by the six sponsoring ADN programs to receive specific support services (i.e., regional workshops, conferences, consultation), and compares these findings to those of all other ADN programs in the U.S. responding to the 1991 and 1993 surveys.

The Nursing Home as a Clinical Learning Setting

The use of the Nursing Home for clinical teaching increased markedly during the Project's duration. The proportion of programs participating in regional dissemination activities reporting student clinical experiences in the Nursing Home during either the 1st or 2nd year of their programs increased significantly by the end of the Project, from 75 percent in 1991 to 90 percent in 1993. The national sample shows a moderate increase, from 74 percent in 1991 to 82 percent in 1993.

Reflecting the Project's emphasis on the value of a 2nd-year clinical experience in the Nursing Home, the participating programs also showed a notable significant increase in the proportion reporting a 2nd-year experience, from 19 percent in 1991 to 57 percent in 1993. Nationally, the proportion increased from 19 percent to 27 percent.

First-year Nursing Home clinical placements likewise increased by the end of the Project. The proportion of participating programs placing first-year students in the Nursing Home increased from 64 percent in 1991 to 75 percent in 1993. Nationally, the proportion increased slightly, from 66 percent to 70 percent.

The proportion of participating programs reporting clinical experiences in other long-term-care (LTC) settings, such as rehabilitation, mental health, and skilled nursing care facilities, increased slightly, from 26 percent in 1991 to 33 percent in 1993. The national increase was somewhat less, from 27 to 30 percent.

A greater proportion of both samples reported the use of *either* the Nursing Home or other LTC settings in their programs in 1993, with the participating programs increasing from 83 to 90 percent and the national sample increasing from 75 to 86 percent.

Learning Experiences Focusing on Well Elderly Adults

The proportion of participating programs reporting a clinical or field experience that focuses on the well elderly increased from 36 percent in 1991 to 52 percent in 1993. Nationally, the proportion of programs reporting well-elderly experiences increased from 29 percent in 1991 to 39 percent in 1993.

The following table details the preceding summarized responses from 95 percent of the 129 participating "regional" programs in 1991 and 68 percent of them in 1993. The national sample of other ADN programs is comprised of 78 percent of 666 such programs surveyed in 1991 and 58 percent of 689 programs surveyed in 1993.

	1991		1993	
	Reg	**Natl**	**Reg**	**Natl**
Programs with 1st-year nursing home clinical experience	64%	66%	75%	70%
Length of 1st-year nursing home clinical experience				
< 6 days	24%	31%	22%	32%
6–10 days	44%	35%	33%	43%
> 10 days	32%	34%	45%	25%
Average No. Days	10	10	11	9
Programs with 2nd-year nursing home clinical experience	19%	19%	57%	27%
Length of 2nd-year nursing home clinical experience				
< 6 days	39%	44%	38%	41%
6–10 days	45%	41%	37%	36%
> 10 days	16%	14%	25%	23%
Average No. Days	7	7	9	8
Programs with either 1st- or 2nd-year nursing home clinical experiences	75%	74%	90%	82%
Programs with other LTC clinical experiences in either 1st or 2nd Year	26%	36%	33%	39%
Programs with either nursing home or other LTC clinical experiences in 1st or 2nd Year	83%	75%	90%	86%
Programs with Well Elderly Learning Experiences	36%	29%	52%	39%

Classroom Hours Addressing Gerontological Nursing Content Areas

The 1991 and 1993 surveys also sought to determine the amount of classroom time that addresses selected topics in gerontological nursing. In spite of difficulties in quantifying time spent on the 12 identified content areas in an integrated curriculum, the following findings, recognizing the limitations of the estimated data, provide a general picture of gerontological nursing in the ADN classroom in 1990–1991 and 1992–1993.

Average Number of Classroom Hours Addressing Content Areas

Content Area	1991		1993	
	Reg	Natl	Reg	Natl
Demographics of aging	.6	.8	.6	.7
Attitudes toward aging	1.2	1.2	1.1	1.0
Theories of aging	.8	.8	.7	.8
Normal physical changes	2.3	2.3	1.9	2.0
Normal psychological changes	1.9	1.7	1.2	1.5
Socio-cultural aspects	1.1	1.2	.9	1.0
Nursing process/Elderly client	3.5	2.7	1.8	2.3
Common health problems	5.2	4.4	3.7	3.8
Community resources	.8	.8	1.0	1.0
Nursing home setting	1.0	.9	1.3	1.2
Politics of aging	.4	.4	.5	.6
Legal/Ethical aspects	1.0	1.0	.8	.9
TOTAL	16	16	15	14

These findings suggest that the amount of classroom time devoted to gerontological nursing did not increase in those programs participating in regional dissemination activities nor in other ADN programs across the nation. Measurement problems, such as the difficulty of estimating the time alloted to specific content areas in an integrated curriculum, limit the validity of these findings. Nonetheless, both samples show slight to moderate decreases over time in a number of the content areas, and only a few small increases.

In conclusion, this Kellogg-sponsored national dissemination effort was extremely successful in changing how ADN students are prepared to care for the elderly. The Nursing Home and other long-term care settings are now used for clinical teaching in nine out of ten of all ADN programs, and more than one-half of the programs targeted for special support now include a clinical or field experience focusing on the well elderly. Evaluative findings regarding classroom content are of questionable validity, but generally show slight negative changes.

TIME TO CARE: THE NURSING HOME CLINICAL*
Video Evaluation Highlights

The video produced by The Community College-Nursing Home Partnership Project in Spring 1991 effectively depicts the Why, What, and How students learn in the nursing home. This judgment comes from 742 faculty, students, nursing home personnel, and other agency staff participating in the evaluation study of the video conducted under the direction of Helen A. Hanson, RN, PhD, project evaluation consultant. These respondents credit the video with providing a rationale for incorporating nursing home clinical teaching in the ADN curriculum and giving examples of What and How students learn in the nursing home.

In the evaluation study, individuals attending one of fourteen conferences and seminars held during May and June across the United States completed a brief questionnaire prior to and following screenings of the video. ADN students enrolled in two Partnership programs also viewed the video and completed the questionnaire as part of a classroom experience before their first clinical experience in a nursing home.

The study concludes that TIME TO CARE successfully portrays the nursing home as an appropriate, positive clinical learning environment that has special value for teaching six particular nursing competencies: management of the environment, rehabilitative nursing skills, assessment, supervisory skills, making judgments based on nursing analysis of care needs, and understanding the care of frail, older adults. More than 96 percent of the respondents agreed, after viewing the video, that the nursing home is an opportune place to teach each of these competencies. The video also changed the views of AD faculty about teaching supervision in the nursing home. The proportion of AD faculty who agreed that the nursing home is an opportune place to teach supervision increased significantly, from 93 percent before the screening to 98 percent afterward. Other highlights from the evaluation study include:

- *100 percent of nursing home personnel and 99 percent of AD faculty agreed that the nursing home holds potential as a setting for clinical teaching.*

---

* First published in the Community College-Nursing Home Project newsletter. *Newslink*, Winter 1992.

- 80 percent of all respondents believed that ADN programs have a community-focussed mission and therefore have a responsibility to prepare graduates for roles in nursing homes.

- AD faculty (97 percent) were more likely than AD students (88 percent) to report that the video made them feel more positive toward teaching in the nursing home.

Participants in the evaluation study also expressed their opinions about specific audiences who would benefit from the video. Nine out of ten respondents indicated that the video would be useful for orienting students to a nursing home clinical learning experience, and 84 percent reported that it would contribute to orienting faculty to clinical teaching in the nursing home. Approximately three-fourths of the respondents thought that nursing home staff and administrators would find the video useful, and two-thirds recommended its use in orienting college administrators and program advisory committees to the nursing home as a clinical affiliation agency.

TIME TO CARE can be expected to play a key role in the next few years in the Partnership Project's dissemination efforts to improve the teaching of gerontological nursing to undergraduate nursing students. Thanks to funds from the Kellogg Foundation, each ADN program should now have its own complimentary copy of the video, and others may obtain a copy from the National League for Nursing.

THE SEQUENCE OF CURRICULUM CHANGE IN GERONTOLOGY:* FACULTY FIRST

Helen A. Hanson and Verle Waters

The aging of the American population is on the mind of most nursing educators today. Faculty are considering, if not yet acting on, the question of how the learning experiences of students will be adapted to meet the needs of an aging population. Many schools are adding to or strengthening instruction related to health care for the elderly.

Typically, a faculty decides that demographic changes contributing to the large number of ill and frail elderly, along with health delivery changes such as the shift of care from acute hospitals to extended care settings, call for curriculum modification. It is not clear, however, what should be changed or how to go about the changes, only that the health care needs of the elderly demand greater attention in the academic program. Spier and Yurick (1981), for example, describe nursing student attitudes toward older patients and recommend curricular approaches to change student attitudes. Brower (1985) and Gioella (1986) outline content topics that they believe are essential for inclusion in the basic educational program. Mezey et al. (1989) describe the methods and benefits of a teaching nursing home for graduate nursing education and nursing research. Prior to the project reported upon here, nursing discourse was silent on the subject of the teaching of gerontologic nursing in the associate degree curriculum.

In 1986, six associate degree programs initiated an answer-seeking approach to curricular change for improving care of the aging population. A four-year demonstration project funded by the W. K. Kellogg Foundation supported establishment of partnerships between six geographically-dispersed ADN programs and one or more nursing homes and other long-term care agencies in each program's locale. The goals of these partnership demonstration centers were: 1) to develop nursing potential in long-term care settings through inservice education, and 2) to influence the redirection of associate degree nursing education to include active

* First published in *Nursing and Health Care, 12,* pp. 516–519.
In this report of a national W. K. Kellogg-supported project designed to strengthen gerontology in the ADN curriculum, Hanson and Waters summarize faculty, curriculum and student outcomes of The Community College-Nursing Home Partnership Project.

preparation for nursing roles in long-term care settings as well as in acute care settings. Operational objectives derived from these two goals served as the evaluation criteria for all project activities and provided the framework for the project implementation and evaluation plans developed by each of the six partnerships.

The operational objectives focused on: 1) communication mechanisms between each program and its nursing home partners that produced cooperative activities aimed at improving the quality of patient care; 2) faculty development in gerontological nursing; 3) curriculum analysis and change that increased program emphasis on gerontological nursing; and 4) student knowledge and attitudes about aging and interest in gerontological nursing as a career choice.

The purpose of this article is to describe the extent to which the demonstration project achieved its intended faculty, curriculum, and student outcomes. Another report (Carignan, submitted for publication) addresses the impact of the communication mechanisms and other partnership activities on professional and non-professional care givers in nursing homes. Additionally, Mengel, et al. (1990) studied the process and ingredients of cooperation between nursing programs and long-term care facilities. Their Delphi study identified characteristics of a successful community college-nursing home partnership, including realistic, achievable and practical partnership goals, and clear, written expectations regarding students' clinical experiences. Other project outcomes, including curriculum modifications and teaching strategies developed within the demonstration projects, are also reported elsewhere (Tagliareni et al., 1991; Waters, 1991).

Given these and other positive outcomes of the demonstration project, which ended in 1990, the W. K. Kellogg Foundation funded a three-year dissemination effort wherein other nursing faculty can learn how they might go about improving the teaching of gerontological nursing. Regional and national workshops, a videotape, and a curriculum guidebook will disseminate lessons learned during the demonstration phase of the project.*

---

* The National League for Nursing is co-producing the national workshops, videotape, and curriculum guidebook. For information about dates and availability, contact NLN.

FACULTY OUTCOMES

Recognizing that faculty are the key to curricular change and the vehicle for affecting the knowledge and attitudes of the next generation of nurses, initial project activities focused on faculty development in gerontological nursing. Each ADN program supported a variety of professional development activities for its own faculty designed to change faculty knowledge about and attitudes toward aging. These activities included on-campus and retreat workshops and conferences, support of conference attendance and enrollment in gerontological courses at nearby universities.

The evaluation plan identified two methods to measure faculty knowledge and attitudes about aging at the beginning and at the end of the demonstration project: 1) the gerontological nursing credentials of the faculty; and 2) the instruments, one measuring knowledge about aging, *Facts on Aging* (Palmore, 1988), and the other assessing attitudes toward older people, *Old People's Scale* (Kogan, 1961).

Table 1 shows that significant changes occurred in the gerontological nursing credentials of the nursing faculty of the six participating programs. Between 1987 and 1990, the proportion of faculty holding ANA certification in gerontological nursing increased significantly, from one to

Table 1
Percent of Faculty in Six Project Programs
with Special Preparation in Geriatrics/Gerontology
Before and After Demonstration Project

Preparation	% Before	% After	$X^2(1df)$	p
15 or more units in field of Gerontology	5%	1%	2.53	.112
Geriatric Nurse Practitioner	0%	2%	1.06	.302
Master's Degree in Gerontological Nursing	3%	6%	0.74	.391
1 or more years of full-time experience in LTC	4%	6%	0.58	.447
ANA certification in Gerontological Nursing	1%	15%	16.81	.000
Completed GEC program of study	0%	19%	25.65	.000

15 percent. Also, the proportion of faculty who had completed a Geriatric Education Center (GEC) program of study increased significantly, from zero to 19 percent. Slight increases occurred in the proportion of faculty holding master's degrees in gerontological nursing, who are certified Geriatric Nurse Practitioners, and who have at least one year of full-time work experience in long-term care.

Consequently, in the six ADN programs employing a total of 156 full- and part-time faculty in 1990, 24 faculty held ANA certification in gerontological nursing, 29 had completed a GEC program of study, and nine held a master's degree in gerontological nursing.

Both at project initiation and termination, faculty completed two instruments commonly used to assess factual knowledge about aging (*Facts on Aging*) and negative stereotyping of the aged (*Old People's Scale*). The matched scores of nursing faculty completing these instruments in 1987 and again in 1990 show no significant difference. In other words, faculty members employed throughout the duration of the project did not demonstrate a significant change in their knowledge and attitudes about aging, according to the two instruments. However, when the 1990 average scores of all faculty employed at that time (N = 95) are compared to those of all faculty in 1987 (N = 100), a significant increase in knowledge of aging is found in scores on *Facts on Aging, Part II* (t = 2.77, df_{171}, p = 0.006). This increase between the 1987 and 1990 scores of the unmatched sample, when viewed in light of increases in the gerontological credentials of faculty, suggests that new faculty joining the programs after 1987 may have influenced this finding.

CURRICULUM OUTCOMES

Between 1987 and 1990, the six programs markedly increased the gerontological nursing components of their curriculum in terms of theory hours, clinical hours, and teaching materials. (See Table 2.) The average number of theory hours addressing the well elderly tripled. The average number of theory hours focusing on the ill elderly as seen in acute care hospitals increased 67 percent. The average number of theory hours addressing the ill/frail elderly as seen in long-term care facilities doubled. Each program instituted its changes following an analysis of the overall curriculum which resulted in a redefinition and reorganization of existing content.

Table 2
Gerontological Components of the Curriculum
of the Six Project Programs, Before and After Project

Curricular Component	Before	After	% Change
Mean number theory hours addressing:			
Well elderly	3	9	+200%
Acutely ill elderly	9	15	+67%
Frail elderly	1	2	+100%
Mean number clinical hours focusing on ill elderly:			
in acute care hospitals	56	80	+43%
in nursing homes	51	73	+43%
in other LTC settings	7	42	+500%
Mean number clinical hours focusing on well elderly	4	14	+250%
Mean number of movies/videotapes focusing on older adults	4	17	+325%

The number of clinical hours that students spend with gerontological clients showed similar gains. The average number of clinical hours focusing primarily on ill elderly patients in acute care hospitals increased 43 percent. Clinical hours focusing primarily on ill elderly in nursing homes also increased 43 percent, and clinical hours focusing on ill elderly in other long-term care settings increased sixfold, or 500 percent. Also, the average number of clinical hours addressing the well elderly increased three and one-half times, or 250 percent. The six programs quadrupled their use of movies and videotapes related to older adults.

Further evidence of curricular change is found in the results of a survey of ADN faculty in the participating programs conducted in 1987 and repeated in 1990. Analysis of the pre- and post-project surveys shows significant increases in the proportion of faculty who believe that their curriculum: 1) includes learning experiences that serve to change negative stereotypes of the aged (54 percent before and 80 percent after); 2) does not emphasize "cure values" at the expense of "care values" (48 percent before and 77 percent after); and 3) includes "positive" learning experiences in nursing homes (51 percent before and 85 percent after).

STUDENT OUTCOMES

The implicit goal of the project's faculty and curriculum development activities was to produce changes in students, both in their knowledge about and attitudes toward the elderly and in their interest in gerontological nursing as a career choice.

Following their enrollment in the six ADN programs, students graduating in 1990 show significant changes in knowledge and attitudes about aging, using the same measurement tools completed by the faculty. Analysis of matched scores of almost 300 graduates obtained at program entrance in 1988 and at graduation in 1990 reveals significant increases in average scores on *Facts on Aging, Part I* ($t = 7.57$, df_{292}, $p = 0.000$) and *Facts on Aging, Part II*, ($t = 1.94$, df_{242}, $p = 0.053$). Furthermore, when scores of the 1990 graduates on this instrument were compared to students graduating from the six programs in 1987 before implementation of curricular changes, the 1990 graduates scored significantly higher on both parts of the *Facts on Aging*. In addition to the significant gain in knowledge about aging between entrance and graduation, the students graduating in 1990 also showed a significant decrease in negative attitudes toward older people, as measured by the *Old People's Scale* ($t = -2.77$, df_{288}, $p = 0.006$).

To assess student interest in gerontological nursing as a career choice, entrance and graduation surveys queried students regarding their preferred post-graduation work setting. Actual work setting selected by graduating students was obtained at graduation. The proportion of 1990 graduates from the six partnership programs indicating that their first or second preference of work setting was a nursing home or convalescent facility increased from seven percent at program entrance to 11 percent at graduation. In an attempt to account for salary and other differences between acute care hospitals and nursing homes, students were also asked to indicate their choice of post-graduation work setting given the hypothetical situation of equal salary and work shift at all types of work settings. Under these conditions, the proportion of 1990 graduates reporting that a nursing home or convalescent facility would be a first or second choice increased from 10 percent at program entrance to 13 percent at graduation. Neither of these modest changes in preferred work setting is statistically significant. However, when the 1990 graduates are compared to the 1987 graduates on actual choice of employment setting, considered a more meaningful variable, 10 percent of the 1990 graduates and only four percent of the 1987 graduates had accepted a position in a nursing home or convalescent facility at the time of graduation.

SUMMARY AND DISCUSSION

In summary, evaluative findings support the conclusion that the project achieved its intended outcomes regarding: 1) faculty knowledge about and attitudes toward aging; 2) curriculum emphasis on gerontological nursing; and 3) student knowledge about aging and interest in working in long-term care facilities. The findings indicate that planned faculty development activities, especially those that lead to gerontological nursing credentials, have a positive effect on faculty knowledge of and attitudes toward care of elderly people. The gain in faculty mean scores on the instruments used is believed to be at least in part attributable to the fact that new faculty hired after the start of the project were more likely to have a degree in gerontology and, assumably, hold more positive attitudes toward working with older people. This is an interesting finding, in that the partnership programs made no concerted effort to recruit gerontologic nurses during this period. It appears that the existence of the nursing home project brought the colleges a faculty applicant pool more gerontologically oriented. Anecdotal accounts from the program administrators regarding faculty hiring during this period substantiate this speculation.

The changes in faculty opinions about the preparation of ADN graduates for roles in nursing homes is a finding that has implications for educators who wish to initiate curricular changes despite reluctance and doubt on the part of some faculty members. At the close of the project, 80 percent of the faculty in the partnership programs agreed that the curriculum changes, which included increased time and attention given to clinical education in the nursing home, provided learning experiences that serve to change negative stereotypes of the aged. Moreover, by the end of the project, the percentage of faculty who believe that their curriculum includes positive learning experiences in nursing homes increased from 51 percent to 85 percent. These findings suggest that the very experience of carrying out curriculum changes to prepare ADN graduates for nursing home roles increases the value faculty attribute to learning experiences in the nursing home.

Both the faculty changes and the marked increase in gerontological nursing instruction in each of the six programs must be viewed as factors influencing the reported student outcomes. The project had an effect on student knowledge of aging and a documented change in their attitudes toward the elderly occurred, findings that complement the increase in student interest in working with older adults. The finding that ten percent of the 1990 graduates accepted positions in nursing homes and convalescent facilities is noteworthy, especially since only four percent of the same programs' 1987 graduates had done so. The assumption can certainly be made that, given the nursing shortage in the spring of 1990, the 1990 graduates did not choose employment in long-term care facilities because they could not obtain positions in acute care facilities. Moreover, experience has led nursing faculty to believe that, with a positive educational experience with the elderly, many new graduates will select long-term care employment after a few years of experience in acute care hospitals. Consequently, these program faculty believe that strengthening gerontological nursing in the curriculum better prepares graduates for nursing practice in today's acute care settings and that such experience will indisputably add to their value when these nurses choose to make their contribution to improving the care of the elderly in nursing homes and other long-term care settings.

REFERENCES

Brower, H. T. (1985). Knowledge competencies in gerontological nursing. In *Overcoming the bias of ageism in long-term care*, (pp. 55–82). New York: The National League for Nursing Press.

Carignan, A. Partnership impact on nursing home care. Submitted for publication to *Geriatric Nursing*.

Gioella, E. C. (1986). Gerontological content for basic professional nursing preparation. In *Gerontology in the professional nursing curriculum*, (pp. 11–27). New York: The National League for Nursing Press.

Kogan, N. (1961). Attitudes toward old people: The development of a scale and an examination of correlates. *Journal of Abnormal and Social Psychology*, 62(1), 44–54.

Mengel, A., Simson, S., Sherman, S., & Waters, V. (1990). Essential factors in a community college-nursing home partnership. *Journal of Gerontological Nursing*, 16(11), 26–31.

Mezey, M. D., Lynaugh, J. E., & Cartier, M. M. (Eds.) (1989). *Nursing homes and nursing care: Lessons from the teaching nursing homes*. New York: Springer.

Palmore, E. B. (1988). *The Facts on Aging Quiz: A handbook of uses and results.* New York: Springer.

Spier, B. E., & Yurick, A. G. (1981). A curriculum design to influence positive student behaviors towards the elderly. *Nursing and Health Care,* 10(5), 265–268.

Tagliareni, E., Sherman, S., Mengel, A., & Waters, V. (1991). Participatory clinical education: Reconceptualizing the clinical learning environment. *Nursing and Health Care,* 12(5), 248–250, 261–263.

Waters, V. (Ed.) (1991). *Teaching gerontology.* New York: The National League for Nursing Press.

Appendix C
Annotated Bibliography of Project Publications

BIBLIOGRAPHY OF PROJECT PUBLICATIONS

1988–1994

Anderson, M. A., Aird, T., & Haslam, B. (1991). How satisfied are nursing home staff? *Geriatric Nursing*, March/April, 85–87.

> Results of a 12 nursing home survey on staff job satisfactions. Identifies factors contributing to job satisfaction.

Anderson, M. A., Beaver, K. W., & Wheeler, R. E. (1991). *The long-term care nursing assistant training manual*. Baltimore: Health Professions Press.

> Written by project faculty at Weber State University, the basis for the text is human needs, maintenance goals, and quality of life issues. Each chapter contains objectives, self-directed learning experiences, essential vocabulary, and interventions to provide basic nursing care to older adults.

Anderson, M. A., & Cobe, G. (1993). The prospective of long-term care educational partnerships: An essential community collaboration, *Prospectives: Celebrating 40 years of associate degree nursing education*. New York: National League for Nursing Press.

> Explores faculty and student learning in a long-term care experience for nursing students through use of student stories. Highlights the advantages of a partnership between nursing homes and community colleges.

Associate degree nursing and the nursing home. (1998). New York: National League for Nursing Press.

> Proceedings from the first national conference sponsored by the Community College-Nursing Home Partnership. Includes articles by project staff addressing partnerships between nursing and nursing home staff and residents, clinical learning environments in long-term care, faculty, students and caregiver attitudes toward the aged and faculty and professional staff development in the nursing home.

Bentz, P., & Ellis, J. (1993). Developing management skills through a preceptor-based experience in community nursing homes. *Prospectives: Celebrating 40 years of associate degree nursing education*. New York: National League for Nursing Press.

Discussion of the preceptor based management experience at Shoreline Community College, including roles of student, faculty and preceptor and methodologies for staff and site selection.

Burke, M., & Sherman, S. (Eds.). (1993). *Gerontological nursing: Issues and Opportunities for the twenty-first century.* New York: National League for Nursing Press.

Proceedings from the national conference sponsored by the Community College-Nursing Home Partnership, Georgetown University and the NLN. Papers address gerontologic nursing from educational, clinical and political perspectives and describe nursing competency development, effective teaching strategies, and new practice models in long-term care.

Burke, M., & Sherman, S. (Eds.). (1993). *Ways of knowing and caring for older adults.* New York: National League for Nursing Press.

Proceedings from the second annual gerontological nursing symposium sponsored by the partnership, Georgetown University, and the NLN. Papers review research in gerontological nursing and illuminate the contrast between traditional science and the naturalistic/ interpretive approach. Includes examples of gerontological nursing practice that derive from empirical trial and error approaches. Applications to nursing education are presented.

Carignan, A. (1992). Community college-nursing home partnership: Impact on nursing care. *Geriatric Nursing, 13,* 273–275.

Reports the results of a survey of directors of nursing in project-affiliated nursing homes, describes the impact of partnership activities on nursing home staff and on caregiving practices.

Carignan, A., & Sherman, S. (1992). Nurse education partnerships benefit facilities and colleges. *Provider, 18,* (1), 33–34.

Discusses the impact of the communication mechanisms and other partnership activities on professional and non-professional caregivers in the nursing home.

Council of Associate Degree Programs. (1992). *Educational outcomes of associate degree programs: Roles and competencies.* New York: National League for Nursing Press.

Publication by the council describing competencies as provider of care, manager of care, and member within the discipline of nursing for the AD nurse at graduation and six months after graduation. This document represents the first specific reference to caring for the older adult as a critical knowledge base in the education of the Associate Degree nurse.

Gerontology in the nursing curriculum. (1992). New York: National League for Nursing Press.

Reports the results of the National Invitational Consensus Conference to identify gerontological nursing competencies for Baccalaureate and Master's degree students. Includes papers by project staff describing strategies and goals for clinical education in the nursing home.

Hanson, H. A., & Waters, V. (1991). The sequence of curriculum change in gerontology: Faculty first. Nursing and Health Care 12, (10), 516–519.

Summarizes faculty, curriculum and student outcomes of the demonstration phase of the Community College-Nursing Home Project, 1986–1990. Emphasizes the need for faculty development as a first step in curriculum change.

Hartley, C., Bentz, P., & Ellis, J. (In press.) The effect of early nursing home placement on student attitudes toward the elderly. Journal of Nursing Education.

Examines the benefits of placing students in nursing homes early in the program of study.

Mengel, A., Simson, S., Sherman, S., & Waters, V. (1991). Essential factors in a community college-nursing home partnership. Journal of Gerontological Nursing, 16, (11), 26–31.

Describes the results of a Delphi study which identified characteristics of a successful partnership between a nursing home and community college nursing programs. Characteristics include realistic, achievable and practical partnership goals and clearly written expectations for student clinical experiences.

Sherman, S. (1993). The community college-nursing home partnership. Determining the future of gerontological nursing education. New York: National League for Nursing Press.

Overview of activities and outcomes of the project, discussion of creative strategies and alliances to enhance learning in gerontological nursing.

Sherman, S. (1988). Models in associate degree nursing program for long-term care. Strategies for long-term care (395–408). New York: National League for Nursing Press.

Describes the curriculum plan developed at the Community College of Philadelphia and includes an overview of project goals and objectives; emphasizes strategies for integrating gerontological nursing content.

Sherman, S., & Waters, V. (1994). Community college-nursing home partnership: Successful strategies for change in nursing education. In McCloskey, J. & Grace, H., (Eds.), *Current issues in nursing* (4th ed.). St. Louis: Mosby Yearbook Inc.

Presents an account of successful curriculum change in associate degree education in the space of a few years, notable because the change meant confronting personal and professional biases about old people and nursing homes.

Simmons, M. E. (1987). College RN curriculum to include long-term care. *Today's Nursing Home, 8*, (8), 3–4.

Describes new curriculum at Triton College in relation to national project goals.

Tagliareni, E. (1993). Issues and recommendations for associate degree education in gerontological nursing. *Determining the future of gerontological nursing education*. New York: National League for Nursing Press.

Outlines goals and implementation strategies for AD curriculum to include individualization of care to older adults and use of long-term care facilities for experience in planning and implementing care directed toward promotion of optimal functional ability. Advocates active engagement of AD faculty in finding new approaches to integration of gerontological nursing in curriculum.

Tagliareni, E. (1993). Creating the future: The story of a teacher-student partnership. *Prospectives: Celebrating 40 years of associate degree nursing education*. New York: National League for Nursing Press.

Keynote address at the NLN-CADP annual meeting. Describes the qualities of the student-teacher relationship in AD Nursing education, illustrated by clinical education in long-term care settings.

Tagliareni, E., Sherman, S., Waters, V., & Mengel, A. (1991). Participatory clinical education: Reconceptualizing the clinical learning environment, *Nursing and Health Care, 12*, (5), 248–250, 261–263.

Reports curriculum modifications and teaching strategies developed within the demonstration projects. Emphasizes the role transition experienced by faculty as they move from acute to long-term care teaching environments.

Waters, V. (1990). Associate degree nursing and curriculum revolution II. *Journal of Nursing Education, 29*, (7), 322–325.

> Review of forty years of AD nursing education and a call for innovative teaching strategies to include gerontology and other settings outside the acute care hospital.

Waters, V. (1988). The community college's role in long term care education. *Strategies for long-term care* (389–394) New York: National League for Nursing Press.

> Description of national project goals and objectives, detailing faculty development, nursing home staff education and curriculum design.

Waters, V. (In press, publication scheduled 1995). *The narrative enlarging: A biography of the community college-nursing home partnership.* New York: National League for Nursing Press.

> An analysis of factors, including project design, organization and implementation that influenced the extent to which project outcomes were achieved.

Waters, V. (1993). The National League for Nursing's initiatives in gerontological nursing education. *Determining the future of gerontological nursing education.* New York: National League for Nursing Press.

> Describes NLN's positions and programs to improve education and practice in gerontological nursing.

Waters, V. (Ed.) (1994). *Resources for teaching gerontology.* New York: National League for Nursing Press.

> Experiential learning activities and annotated references to print and film media which help in teaching gerontological nursing.

Waters, V. (1991). (Ed.). *Teaching Gerontology.* New York: National League for Nursing Press.

> Written by project faculty, the text explores the essential gerontological knowledge and skills needed to practice nursing today. Authors highlight the rich learning environment found in nursing homes, and suggest models for effective partnerships between community colleges and nursing homes. Appendix includes sample learning activities tested in project schools.

PUBLICATIONS BY STUDENTS

Students who participated in learning activities during the project years write about their experiences knowing and caring for older adults.

Alston, L., Dempsey, H-M., Franklin, C., McGonagle, S., Moore, T., Rowland, S., & Tagliareni, E. (1989). Care technique for elderly clients. *Advancing Clinical Care*, 16–18.

Bedard, S. (1991). Coat hangers to learning. *Imprint*, 38, (1), 61–63.

Burke, A., Shirley, E., Baker, C., Deno, L., & Tagliareni, E. (1990). Perceptions from the nursing home: How we can make a difference. *Imprint*, 37, (4), 62–65.

Pagano-Victor, C. (1990). Walking with Carmella. *Nursing Homes*, 39, (2), 19–20.

Perlstein, K. (1992). Interview with a well older adult: A nursing student's perspective. *Geriatric Nursing*, 14, (1), 36–38.

NON-PRINT MEDIA

Waters, V. (Executive Producer), & Ely, T. (Director). (1991). *Time to care: The nursing home clinical.* Videotape. New York: National League for Nursing.

Appendix D
Survey Forms, "Project Principals' Perceptions"

PROJECT PRINCIPALS' PERCEPTIONS OF FACTORS CONTRIBUTING TO PROJECT SUCCESS

The purpose of this questionnaire is to obtain from the key players in The Community College-Nursing Home Partnership Project their perceptions of the project's achievements and what contributed to them. It asks you to share your personal views about the grant experience from the time of first funding. Candor and thoughtfulness are requested rather than polished prose. Use separate sheets of paper (or start on the reverse of this one), and you may identify each question by number only. (No need to recopy the question.) Please take your time and answer as fully as possible. No answer will be too long! Please return to Verle Waters (16 Chestnut Ave., Los Gatos, CA 95030) between March 1 and May 1, 1993.

Please indicate your role in the Kellogg project:

_____Nursing Program Administrator

_____Project Coordinator

_____Faculty with Project Assignment(s)

Specify type of Assignment(s):_____

Please state the dates (time period) of your participation in the project:

_____

1. *Looking at the full span of the project from the demonstration through dissemination phases, discuss factors that helped and interfered with how your site addressed each of the areas of project focus listed below. For each area of project focus, please consider such factors as: structure, people involved, strategies employed, leadership and direction, and alliances and connections.*

   Areas of focus:

   —*Faculty Development*

   —*New Nursing Home Affiliations*

   —*Staff Development in Nursing Homes*

   —*Increasing Gerontological Nursing Content in Program*

—*Establishing Second-Year Nursing Home Clinical Practicum*

—*Other (Specify as many as you wish)*

2. In terms of your college's partnership with a nursing home, discuss the factors that facilitated and hindered the development and maintenance of a "partner" relationship. (For example, was the relationship facilitated by any special agreements or arrangements, or any particular communication strategies, or anything done by either party that promoted cooperative efforts? And, was the "partner" relationship hindered by any particular barriers or problems, or unplanned developments at the college or at the nursing home?) Also, in your opinion, what are the essential characteristics of a successful partnership between two structurally unrelated organizations, such as a community college and a nursing home?

3. From your point of view, what are the most significant and lasting aspects of the project, nationally and at your site? Discuss why you believe these aspects have a good chance of lasting.

4. Given that a second-year, long-term care clinical affiliation for nursing students was made a goal in the project, what factors, conditions, and/or elements in your program or nursing home made it possible to bring about this change?

5. What aspects of the project have given you the most satisfaction since the grant began?

6. What other important changes have taken place in your program as a result of the Kellogg grant?

PROJECT PRINCIPALS' PERCEPTIONS OF FACTORS CONTRIBUTING TO PROJECT SUCCESS

The purpose of this questionnaire is to obtain from the key players in The Community College-Nursing Home Partnership Project their perceptions of the project's achievements and what contributed to them. It asks you to share your personal views about the grant experience from the time of first funding. Candor and thoughtfulness are requested rather than polished prose. Use separate sheets of paper (or start on the reverse of this one), and you may identify each question by number only. (No need to re-copy the question.) Please take your time and answer as fully as possible. No answer will be too long! Please return to Verle Waters (16 Chestnut Ave., Los Gatos, CA 95030) between March 1 and May 1, 1993.

Please indicate your role in the Kellogg project:

_____Nursing Home Partner

Specify Position:_____

Specify Role in Project_____

Please state the dates (time period) of your participation in the project:

_____

1. *From your point of view, what are the most significant and lasting aspects of the project, nationally and at your site or facility? Discuss why you believe these aspects have a good chance of lasting.*

2. *In terms of your facility's partnership with a community college, discuss the factors that facilitated and hindered the development and maintenance of a "partner" relationship. (For example, was the relationship facilitated by any special agreements or arrangements, or any particular communication strategies, or anything done by either party that promoted cooperative efforts? And, was the "partner" relationship hindered by any particular barriers or problems, or unplanned developments at the college or at your facility?) Also, in your opinion, what are the essential characteristics of a successful partnership between two structurally unrelated organizations, such as a community college and a nursing home?*

3. Given that a second-year, long-term care clinical affilitation for nursing students was made a goal in the project, what factors, conditions, and/or elements in your facility made it possible to bring about this change?

3. What aspects of the project have given you the most satisfaction since the grant began?

4. What other important changes have taken place in your facility as a result of the Kellogg grant?

PROJECT PRINCIPALS' PERCEPTIONS OF FACTORS CONTRIBUTING TO PROJECT SUCCESS

The purpose of this questionnaire is to obtain from the key players in The Community College-Nursing Home Partnership Project their perceptions of the project's achievements and what contributed to them. It asks you to share your personal views about the grant experience from the time of first funding. Candor and thoughtfulness are requested rather than polished prose. Please take your time and answer as fully as possible. No answer will be too long! Please return to Verle Waters (16 Chestnut Ave., Los Gatos, CA 95030) between March 1 and May 1, 1993.

Please indicate your role in the Kellogg project:

_____National Advisory Committee Member

_____Local Project Advisory Committee Member

Please state the dates (time period) of your participation in the project:

_____

1. *Given the success of this project, we are attempting to obtain perspectives of those involved regarding what contributed to and interfered with project implementation. Please comment on your perspective of: 1) project structure and organization, and 2) implementation strategies influencing project operation.*

Appendix E
Roster of Principal Members of the Project Staff
1986–1993

Connie Allekian, MSN, RN. Triton College
Mary Ann Anderson, MS, RN, CNA. Weber State University
Patricia Bentz, MSN, RNC. Shoreline Community College
Pamela Burton, MS, RN. Weber State University
Ann Carignan, MSN, RNC. Valencia Community College
Carol Casten, MSN, RN. (Deceased) Triton College
Gail M. Cobe, MSN, RN. Ohlone College
Ivory C. Coleman, MSN, RN. Community College of Philadelphia
Marilee Culhane, MSN, RN. Triton College
Janice Ellis, PhD, RN. Shoreline Community College
Gerry L. Hansen, EdD, RN. Weber State University
Helen A. Hanson, PhD, RN. Project Evaluator
Celia L. Hartley, MN, RN. Shoreline Community College
Gloria Kuhlman, DNS, RN. Ohlone College
Joan Libner, MS, RN. Triton College
Sharlene Limon, MS, RN. Ohlone College
Andrea Mengel, PhD, RN. Community College of Philadelphia
Ann Miller, MA, RNC. Valencia Community College
Susan Sherman, MA, RN. Community College of Philadelphia
Mary Ellen Simmons, MS, RNC. Triton College
Elaine Tagliareni, MS, RNC. Community College of Philadelphia
Verle Waters, MA, RN. Ohlone College
Ruth Y. Webb, EdD, RN. Valencia Community College
Hal White, MS, RN. Valencia Community College

Other Books of Interest from NLN Press

You may order NLN books by • TELEPHONE 800-NOW-9NLN, ext. 138
• Fax 212-989-3710 • MAIL Simply use the order form below

Book Title	Pub. No.	Price	NLN Member Price
☐ **Prospectives: Celebrating 40 Years of Associate Degree Nursing Education** *Edited by Jean A. Simmons*	23-2517	$26.95	$23.95
☐ **Resources for Teaching Gerontology** *By Verle Waters*	14-2608	28.95	25.95
☐ **Teaching Gerontology: The Curriculum Imperative** *Edited by Verle Waters*	15-2411	28.95	25.95
☐ **Gerontological Nursing: Issues and Opportunities for the Twenty-First Century** *Edited by Mary Burke & Susan Sherman*	14-2510	27.95	24.95
☐ **Ways of Knowing and Caring For Older Adults** *Edited by Mary Burke & Susan Sherman*	14-2541	29.95	26.95
☐ **Annual Review of Women's Health, Volume II** *Edited by Beverly McElmurry & Randy Spreen Parker*	19-2669	37.95	34.35
☐ **Health as Expanding Consciousness (2nd ed.)** *By Margaret A. Newman*	14-2626	35.95	32.35
☐ **Nursing Centers: The Time Is Now** *Edited by Barbara Murphy*	41-2629	25.95	22.95

PHOTOCOPY THIS FORM TO ORDER BY MAIL OR FAX

Photocopy this coupon and send with 1) a check payable to NLN, 2) credit card information, or 3) a purchase order number to: **NLN Publications Order Unit, 350 Hudson Street, New York, NY 10014 (FAX: 212-989-3710).**

Shipping & Handling Schedule	
Order Amount	Charges
Up to $24.99	$ 3.75
25.00-49.99	5.25
50.00-74.99	6.50
75.00-99.99	7.75
100.00 and up	10.00

Subtotal: $ _____

Shipping & Handling (see chart): _____

Total: $ _____

☐ Check enclosed   ☐ P.O. # _____   NLN Member # (if appl.): _____

Charge the above total to   ☐ Visa   ☐ MasterCard   ☐ American Express

Acct. #: _____ Exp. Date: _____

Authorized Signature: _____

Name _____ Title _____

Institution _____

Address _____

City, State, Zip _____

Daytime Telephone ( ) _____ Ext. _____

AHm7SanT
82